Eat, Drink & Be Merry

THE BRITISH AT TABLE

1600–2000

Eat, Drink & Be Merry

THE BRITISH AT TABLE
1600–2000

Edited by Ivan Day

YORK CIVIC TRUST

ENGLISH HERITAGE

Norfolk Museums Service

PHILIP WILSON PUBLISHERS · LONDON

Frontispiece:
A modern re-creation of a late baroque dessert (*c.*1749) by Ivan Day and Tony Barton at Fairfax House, York.

Sugar dessert sculptures of this kind often conveyed a symbolic message to the diners. This particular setting is based on the story of Circe, the sorceress who turned Ulysses' men into swine. The significance of an allegory of greed at the finale of the meal would not have been lost on guests who had already consumed two substantial courses of savoury dishes and puddings. (See also figs 31 & 40.)

Front cover: Lithograph by MG, *Fatal Effects of Gluttony – A Lord Mayor's Day Night Mare*

Back cover: Creamware Teapot with transfer printed decoration, possibly Liverpool, *c.*1770. Norfolk Museums Service (Norwich Castle Museum)

The publication of this book accompanies a three-venue touring exhibition:

York, Fairfax House	26 February – 4 June 2000
London, Kenwood House	27 June – 24 September 2000
Norwich, Assembly House	14 October 2000 – 7 January 2001

Editor:	Ivan Day
Editorial Team:	Peter Brown, Andrew Moore, Gillian Riley
Curatorial Team:	Jane Bennett, Peter Brown, Ivan Day, Julia Findlater, Christopher Garibaldi, Andrew Moore
Painting Entries:	Gillian Riley
Essay Contributors:	Peter Brears, Peter Brown, Lisa Chaney, Ivan Day, Laura Mason, Eileen White, C. Anne Wilson

First published in 2000 by Philip Wilson Publishers Ltd
143–149 Great Portland Street, London W1N 5FB
Distributed in the USA and Canada by Antique Collectors' Club, 91 Market Street Industrial Park, Wappingers' Falls, New York 12590

ISBN 0 85667 519 9

Copy-edited and typeset by Helen Robertson
Typeface (Miller) chosen by Gillian Riley
Consultant for painting captions: Gillian Riley
Printed and bound in Italy by Società Editorial Lloyd, Srl, Trieste

Contents

When we Drink our tea
Let us merry be

Preface & Acknowledgements

THE PUBLICATION of this book accompanies a three-venue touring exhibition, *Eat, Drink and Be Merry: The British at Table 1600–2000*, a collaboration between Norfolk Museums Service, the York Civic Trust and English Heritage. The exhibition has been indemnified by Her Majesty's Government under the National Heritage Act 1980 and arranged through the Museums and Galleries Commission and the Department of Culture, Media and Sport. Comprising over thirty important paintings, some four hundred decorative arts objects and numerous culinary masterpieces, all brought together in historic room settings and cased displays, the exhibition helps bring to life in a very tangible way the daily rituals of the British at table.

Food and its presentation at table during any particular period in history is as distinctive as the costume of the time and can reveal as much about the society that created it as contemporary literature or architecture. The driving force behind the creation of this visual feast is a collaboration between food historian Ivan Day, Fairfax House Museum Director Peter Brown and modelmaker Tony Barton, who between them have pioneered the use of contextual displays of this kind in Britain.

Gillian Riley, Andrew Moore, Christopher Garibaldi, Jane Bennett, Julia Findlater and Teresa Fazio-Gannon have also played a significant part in bringing this project to fruition, as have the many members of staff and volunteers at each exhibition venue. Thanks are also due to Anne Jackson and the team at Philip Wilson Publishers for producing a superb publication that will prove a lasting tribute to the welcome collaboration between the York Civic Trust, English Heritage and the Norfolk Museums Service.

Most exhibitions of this nature cannot be assembled from a single museum's collection but rely heavily on the generosity of others in providing material for display. We are particularly grateful to Her Majesty the Queen for so graciously agreeing to lend objects and paintings from the Royal Collection and for permission to quote from correspondence held in the Royal Archives, to His Excellency Mohamed Mahdi Altajir for his kindness and support, and to the following institutions and private individuals who so willingly made treasures from their collections available to us for such a long period. Our thanks are due particularly to: the Ashmolean Museum, Oxford; Bowes Museum; Bradford Art Galleries and Museums; Broadfield House Glass Museum; Bill Brown; John Butler; the Duke of Devonshire and the Chatsworth Settlement Trustees;

FIG. 1
Earthenware teapot decorated with orange slip and underglaze-blue painting, bearing the low-fired gilded inscription:

When we drink our tea
Let us merry be

Possibly made in the Tyneside or Sunderland area, *c.*1785
Height: 14.3 cm

Teapots with messages, mottoes, names and the occasional date are not unusual during this period. However, this cheerful verse, on a pot of unpretentious form and material, conjures up an image not of fashionable high society tea-drinking but of homely fireside conversation.

Guildhall Art Gallery and Library, London; London Transport Museum; Mercer Art Gallery, Harrogate Museums and Arts; Jeanette Hayhurst; David Howard; Ralph Hoyle; Kirklees Metropolitan Council Permanent Collection; Lady Victoria Leatham; Manchester City Art Gallery; James Methuen-Campbell; Minton Museum; David Mitchell; Museen des Mobiliendepots, Vienna; National Portrait Gallery, London; City of Plymouth Museums and Art Gallery; Quernmore Collection; David Redman; Royal Scottish Academy (Diploma Collection); Russell-Cotes Art Gallery and Museum, Bournemouth; Sefton Art Galleries and Museums; Lionel Stopford-Sackville; Tate Gallery, London; Lucien Taylor; Torbay Council (The Torre Abbey Collection); Trustees of All Hallows Church, Harthill; Viscount Windsor; Wedgwood Museum; Wolverhampton Art Gallery; York Minster. To those lenders who choose to remain anonymous we offer our grateful thanks for their selfless generosity.

Among those who freely gave advice, assistance, information and expertise, our grateful thanks go to: Chlöe Archer, David Astley, Sir Nicholas Bacon and the Trustees of the Assembly House, Norwich, Bruce Bailey, Tony Barton, Gay Blake-Roberts, Debbie Brodie, Dominic Brown, Julius Bryant, Sue Buck, John Butler, Caroline Campbell, Howard Coutts, Alan and Jane Davidson, Howard Davies, Sheila De Bellaigue, Roger Dodsworth, Elizabeth Edwards, Brendan Flynn, Hazel Forsyth, Mireille Galinou, Irene Gilchrist, David Gilkeson, Heather Guthrie, Robin Harcourt-Williams, Lisa Heathcote, Christine Hopper, David Howard, Simon Howard, Ralph Hoyle, Ralph Hyde, Joan Jones, Richard Kilburn (who sadly did not live to see this book), Mike King, Vivien Knight, Carla Laithe, Gilly Lehmann, Alf Longhurst, John Malden, Jonathan Marsden, Paul Merry, Charles Noble, Ken Noble, Susan Palmer, Ian Pickford, Corinna Pike, Christopher Pringle, Marcia Reed, Hugh Roberts, Helen Rowles, Stuart Ruddle, GGS Photo Graphics, Maria Sealy, Colin Self, Alistair Smith, George Smith, Christine Stevens, Andrew Stewart, Clive Stewart-Lockhart, Lionel Stopford-Sackville, Sir Roy Strong, Layinka Swinburne, Nicholas Thornton, Julia Trevelyan Oman, Sam Twining, Gerry Webb, Lavinia Wellicome, Gill Whitehead, Harry Williams-Bulkeley and Pamela Wood.

Exhibitions of this nature require much time and energy on the part of those involved in pulling the whole project together. However, no matter how good the idea or how desirable the product, they inevitably flounder without the aid of sponsorship.

We are particularly grateful to our principal sponsor, Waitrose, and also to Asprey & Garrard, Royal Doulton, Twinings, the Friends of Fairfax House, the Noel G. Terry Charitable Trust and Maxiprint, who have made the project possible.

JOHN SHANNON, *Chairman, York Civic Trust*
SIR JOCELYN STEVENS, *Chairman, English Heritage*
AUBREY POBOREFSKI, *Chairman, Norfolk Joint Museums Committee*

ABOUT THE CONTRIBUTORS

Peter Brears is a food historian who was formerly Director of Leeds City Museums. In recent years he has been instrumental in restoring important country house kitchens to their original glory, including those at Petworth and Harewood. His numerous publications include *Traditional Food in Yorkshire* (John Donald, 1987) and *All the King's Cooks* (Souvenir Books, 1999). He is a Sophie Coe Prize winner.

Peter Brown, Director of Fairfax House Museum, York, is a leading authority on eighteenth-century English decorative art. He has a particular interest in table layout and his innovative contextual exhibitions at Fairfax House have explored the relationship between food and the arts. His numerous catalogues include, for the York Civic Trust, *Pyramids of Pleasure* (1990), *In Praise of Hot Liquors* (1995) and *Come Drink the Bowl Dry* (1996).

Lisa Chaney is a writer specializing in food and the fine arts. Her recent biography of Elizabeth David, *Elizabeth David* (Macmillan, 1998), explores the life and work of the most important cookery writer of the second half of the twentieth century, whose influence has had such a profound effect on the shaping of current British attitudes to food.

Ivan Day is a food historian with a special interest in re-creating food of the past in period settings. He has collaborated on several occasions with Peter Brown, most notably on *The Pleasures of the Table* (1997). Other recent exhibitions in England and the United States that have featured his work include *The Tempting Table* (Bowes Museum, 1994), *A Feast for the Eyes* (The Rothschild Collection, Waddesdon Manor, 1998–9), *London Eats Out* (Museum of London, 1999–2000) and *The Edible Monument* (Paul Getty Research Institute, 2000).

Laura Mason is a leading authority on British regional foods. She was responsible for the British contribution to the EU Euroterroirs project. Her findings were recently published in *Traditional Foods of Britain: an Inventory* (Prospect Books, 1999). She is also the author of *Sugar Plums and Sherbet. The Prehistory of Sweets* (Prospect Books, 1998).

Gillian Riley is a food historian and designer with a passion for fine art and typography. Her translation of Giacomo Castelvetro's *The Fruit, Herbs and Vegetables of Italy* (1989) won critical acclaim. She has written many books and papers, including *A Feast for the Eyes* (National Gallery Publications, 1997), and a recent essay in *Food in the Arts* (Prospect Books, 1999) won her the Sophie Coe Prize.

Eileen White is a historian with a special interest is the evolution of the British breakfast. She has been a contributor on more than one occasion to the Leeds History of Food Symposium and is the editor of *Feeding a City* (Prospect Books, 1999), a multi-authored work resulting from the 1996 and 1998 symposia, both of which focused on the history of food in the city of York.

C. Anne Wilson is the organizer of the annual Leeds Food Symposium, which celebrates its tenth anniversary in 2000. Her seminal book *Food and Drink in Britain* (Constable, 1974) remains to this day the single most useful reference work on the subject. Notable among the many other books and papers of which she is the author is *The Book of Marmalade* (Constable, 1985).

FIG. 2
Joseph van Aken (*c.*1699–1749),
Grace before a Meal, *c.*1725
Oil on canvas, 35 × 30 cm

Joseph van Aken chose the right moment to come to England for work. According to Horace Walpole: 'As in England almost everybody's picture is painted, so almost every painter's works were painted by Van Aken.' He made such a comfortable living from painting the drapery and opulent costumes in other artists' portraits that he was able to live in style and become something of an art connoisseur. The members of the family that van Aken depicts here saying grace before a meal have closed, wary countenances, showing none of the cheerful pride and self-confidence so often evident in his society portraits. They are neither rich nor poor; their kitchen is neat and tidy, but far from luxurious with its flagged stone floor and oak boards. Since the dripping pan rests unused behind a spit above the chimney breast, we can assume that the family are sitting down to a simple meal of boiled meat rather than a roast – perhaps farced mutton. Stuffed with fresh herbs and possibly capers, the flesh has a pleasing texture and a delicate pinkish tinge. This dinner of a single food item contrasts markedly with the table plans in contemporary cookery texts, in which lavish meals of many different dishes are proposed. This painting is set firmly in the real world, as most ordinary English families could not have afforded such indulgence. The pewter plates and plain salt-glazed kitchen bowls and jars are a deliberate contrast to the fine oriental china and silver teapot and kettle of the same artist's *English Family at Tea*. These are not folk to commission expensive images of themselves. Rather, they are a reminder of the humble origins and worthy aspirations of many of van Aken's clients.

Introduction

FOOD, the most basic of human needs, has always been one of the great driving forces of mankind, yet historians have rarely considered it an area worthy of study. In recent decades, however, this attitude has begun to change dramatically and a great deal of important work has been published on the social history of British food. C. Anne Wilson's *Food and Drink in Britain* (Constable, 1974) was one of the first serious works to draw attention to the evolution of the British diet. Her interest in the subject was aroused when she worked as a librarian with the rich collection of period cookery books housed in the Brotherton Library at Leeds University.

For a nation that has often been criticized for its poorly developed cuisine, Britain possesses one of the richest legacies of cookery literature of any European country. It has been observed that 'the French and Italians cook, while the English just write about it', but the food described in many of these texts, especially those published before the industrial revolution, demonstrate that at times we have enjoyed a cuisine as good as that of any continental tradition. Many of today's fashionable ingredients, such as rocket and rosewater, were well known in the seventeenth century, when all salad oil was 'extra virgin' and every farmer in the north-east of England ate 'multi-grain' bread.

In 1723, in his *Cook's and Confectioner's Dictionary*, John Nott, one-time cook to the Duke of Bolton, poetically compared England to biblical Canaan: 'so richly is it stor'd with Flesh, Fowl and Fish in an admirable Variety.' It is important to remember, however, that the 'Milk and Honey' of Nott's vision of Canaan did not flow in everybody's direction. We must be cautious of romantic and nationalistic views of our food heritage. Even today, popular studies in the history of gastronomy are beset with inaccurate conceptions of our ancestors' eating habits. Claims (lacking scientific proof) that the Tudors ate bananas and that paw-paw was popular at the Stuart court are recent reminders of how this false mythology of food continues to be propagated in the public imagination.

In addition to the rich archive of cookery books, household accounts and inventories that tell us the real truth about our ancestors' diet, we are fortunate in Britain in having many surviving period kitchens that provide us with important clues about how they cooked their meals. The vast sixteenth-century service wing at Hampton Court Palace is unique in Europe and recent studies carried out there by the food historian Peter Brears have revealed how this factory-like complex prepared meals both for the court and for palace staff (*All the King's Cooks*, Souvenir Press, 1999). Accurate restorations of country house kitchens superintended by Peter Brears at Harewood and Petworth are proving very popular with visitors, who are often able to watch the authentic preparation of period food in an appropriately equipped kitchen environment.

Our understanding of how food was presented at table at different periods has also been increased by a number of recent museum exhibitions and displays. Perhaps one of the most important and revealing of these was *The Tempting Table*, organized at the Bowes Museum by ceramics specialist Howard Coutts in 1994. Contextual displays of tableware and period food have also become an annual event at Fairfax House in York, where visitors have at times been able to admire a complex eighteenth-century dessert at close quarters, or to learn how a place for dinner would have been set at the time of the Regency. Taking precious tableware out of the museum display case and exhibiting it correctly with authentic period food not only brings such objects to life but frequently illuminates our understanding of how they were used.

This policy of allowing history to speak for itself is the underlying premise of the current exhibition and this accompanying book, which celebrate our national meals from the reign of Elizabeth I to that of Elizabeth II. To this end a number of important paintings showing the British at table have been brought together for the first time from a variety of institutions and private collections. Unlike the artists of the Netherlandish school and other continental traditions, British painters have rarely concentrated on details of food; rather, they have tended to focus on the social context of the meal and on the diners themselves. In order to fill in the frequently missing visual clues as to how the food was served, the paintings are displayed alongside faithful re-creations of period settings, with original tableware and authentic food. Case displays of contemporary tableware and napery reinforce this message. This approach makes it possible, for instance, to admire Houckgeest's 1635 painting of King Charles I dining at Whitehall (fig. 34) from the vantage point of a table set out with an authentic seventeenth-century feast. The selection of table settings and historic re-creations present the table fully dressed either for conspicuous consumption or plainly functional eating, depending upon the fashions of the time or the pocket of the consumer.

Much of the food in the table displays – for example, the confectionery – is real and has been made using authentic methods and materials. Models of some dishes, such as the roast birds, have been cast directly from originals that were correctly trussed and roasted on a spit. These displays would not have been possible without the remarkable model-making skills and artistry of Tony Barton.

In the selection of paintings to illuminate the publication we have purposely concentrated on British works of art, which have seldom been considered in the specialist food history literature. Major paintings by lesser-known regional artists, together with masterpieces of national renown, here act as visual testimony to the eating habits of the British at table. Paintings by foreign artists working in England have also been included – as ever, the history of British culture is a story of foreign influence as much as of indigenous taste and fashion. Some works not included in the exhibition are reproduced in the book to illuminate important points made in the text. On the other hand, the book is not a complete catalogue of the works in the exhibition, as some of the paintings on display are not illustrated here. Although a rich seam of material exists in the form of prints, watercolours, photographs and advertising material, space limitations have allowed us to include no more than a few important examples.

In this year of millennium celebrations we have chosen to start by reflecting on meals and foods for special occasions that commemorate important rites of passage and national events. This is followed by a discussion of dinner, our main meal of the day, while subsequent chapters deal with the lesser meals of breakfast and tea and with the perennial British enjoyment of eating in the open air. To conclude, we bring the subject right up to date by examining modern-day trends that govern the choices available for a meal for the millennium.

CHAPTER 1

Feasting & Celebrating

ENTHUSIASTIC and sometimes excessive junketing has always figured as a conspicuous feature of celebrations and festivities in Britain. Whether at a great national feast such as a coronation, a family Christmas dinner or a wedding breakfast, the British love nothing more than to gather and rejoice around a generously laden table. In a treatise on the food and eating habits of his fellow Tudors, the Elizabethan physician Thomas Moufet (1540–1604) remarked:

> *The whole nation of English men delight still in feasting and making of good chear, eating much meat and of many sorts, prolonging their settings with musick and merriments and afterwards sporting themselves in set dances.*[1]

Although the British continue to delight in 'good chear' today, the past four hundred years have brought remarkable changes to the nature of the food and drink we enjoy at our celebratory events. During Moufet's lifetime lavish ceremonial meals, such as those held annually by the London livery companies, were occasions when 'much meat and of many sorts' was certainly the order of the day. Modern ecologically-minded diners would be horrified at the victuals served up to the livery companies' members and aldermen, who traditionally dined on swan, capon and hernshoe (heron), although other birds were consumed with equal relish. A poem of 1579 by Edward Hake, which includes an account of such a City feast, lists bitterns, larks, lapwings, stonechats, bustards, blackbirds and cranes followed by:

> *Straunge kindes of fysh at second course to come in their degree,*
> *As Porpesse, Seale and Samond good, with Sturgeon of the best.*[2]

The word 'straunge' gives us a clue to the appeal of these exotic foods to diners

FIG. 3
The Duke of Newcastle's Feast, after a table plan in Patrick Lamb's *Royal Cookery* (London 1710)

This photograph shows a modern re-creation of the feast set up in the great baroque hall of Castle Howard, Yorkshire. (See also figs 22 & 23.)

FIG. 4 (overleaf)
Joris Hoefnagel (1542–after 1600), *A Wedding Fête at Bermondsey*, c.1570
Oil on panel, 73.8 × 99.2 cm

whose normal daily diet was a mess of pottage followed by 'plain roast and boiled'. Swans and herons, considered to be noble birds, had long been favoured by the aristocracy at high table, a fact that would have given them an added piquancy at gatherings of city grocers, brewers and mercers. There may have been other reasons why these relatively unpalatable creatures were so appreciated. According to Renaissance medical theories, blackbirds and cranes were 'not of a very pleasant taste and smell, but with a certain kind of Acrimony'. Nevertheless they were believed 'to stop Looseness, heal the *Dysentaria* and Cholick and resist the Infection of the Plague'.[3]

We have a clear idea of how these feasts were laid out, since detailed records of the purchase of both food and table equipage have survived. Some livery companies still retain a small amount of pre-Civil War silver in their collections, despite having suffered considerable losses during the Commonwealth. At that time wealthy companies such as the Drapers were obliged to sacrifice over 2,500 ounces of plate, while the Mercers, in need of ready cash, also sold a large quantity. As recorded in the disposals for the years 1642–6, there were several dining pieces – most notably 'one doz. of silver trencher plates' weighing 101½ ounces in 1642, and another 'twelve trencher plates', part of a large quantity of plate sold in 1643. Following the Great Fire of 1666 the Mercers were forced to dispose of most of their plate; only four pieces remain in the Company's collection today.

The nature of festival food and drink served at important family occasions such as weddings has also changed beyond all recognition. Although Elizabethan and Jacobean marriages featured cakes, these bore no resemblance at all to the multi-tiered fantasies popular in the twentieth century.

A rare glimpse into English family life of the 1570s is provided by the Netherlandish artist Joris Hoefnagel, whose painting *A Wedding Fête at Bermondsey* shows us a village marriage procession (fig. 4) in which four gigantic bride cakes are being borne to the wedding feast from the church (see also detail, fig. 5). These extremely large cakes, which probably weighed in the region of 30 lbs apiece, were carried in solemn procession to the church, a custom that had grown out of the pre-Reformation wedding service, during which bread and wine provided by the couple were blessed by the priest. A recipe of 1655 informs us that they were rather like oversized Banbury cakes, heavily perfumed with musk and ambergris.[4] The artist has meticulously painted in a few currants erupting through the crusts, thus confirming that these are indeed great cakes rather than pies or pasties.

The stately procession from the church contains all the elements of an earlier sixteenth-century bridal procession described by Francis Deloney:

> *... then was there a faire Bride cup of silver and gilt carried before her, wherein was a goodly braunch of Rosemarie gilded very faire, hung about with silken Ribonds of all colours; next was there a noyse of Musitians that played all the way before her; afyter her came all the chiefest maydens of the Countrie, some bearing great Bride Cakes.*[5]

FIG. 5
The above detail from Hoefnagel's *Wedding Fête at Bermondsey* (fig. 4) shows four massive 'Banbury cakes' being carried from the church to the wedding feast. These great currant-filled cakes, scented with musk and ambergris, were the rustic forerunners of the modern-day wedding cake. Note also the 'grand sallets', the opening dish of the feast, just visible behind the serving hatch.

The 'faire Bride cup', held aloft by a man preceding the group of nobility (see detail, fig. 6), would have been blessed in the church. Hoefnagel has painted its sprigs of rosemary with exquisite clarity, even down to the mottoes written on the red and white ribbons that adorn them. The table in the room beyond is laid with a fine white cloth scattered with flowers.

At royal weddings, such as that of Elizabeth, the daughter of James I, to the Count Palatine in 1613, delicate wafers, rather than rustic cakes, were eaten by the guests, washed down with hippocras from a great golden bowl.[6]

FIG. 6
In the detail on the left the bride leader holds aloft a gilt bride cup filled with hippocras or muskadine. The handsome rosemary branch is adorned with red and white ribbons and knots emblematic of childbirth and fecundity – red for blood, white for milk.

FIGS 7 & 8
Woodcut bride pie designs taken from Robert May's *Accomplisht Cook* (1660)

Hippocras, a sweet spiced wine, was also the chosen celebratory drink at christenings, at which occasions it was drunk with comfits. These sugar-coated nuts, spices and seeds were a universal festival treat and would be showered over the bride's head at weddings as an emblem of fruitfulness and abundance.

Regional varieties of bride cake survived in parts of the North of England and Scotland until the 1820s, often taking the form of flat oatcakes or currant griddle cakes. By the late eighteenth century the bride cake had evolved in less remote areas into the familiar iced plum cake of the modern wedding reception. However, it stubbornly refused to shake off its ancient links with fecundity and divination. After a gentry wedding in Welford in Berkshire in 1770, small slices of the cake were 'drawn properly thro' the Wedding Ring for the dreaming Emolument of many Spinsters and Batchelors'. An anonymous poem of 1799 tells us that the unmarried friends of the couple slept with a small piece of the charmed cake under their pillow, hoping to dream of their future spouse:

With her own hand she charms each destined slice,
And thro' the ring repeats the trebled thrice.
The hallow'd ring infusing magick power,
Bids Hymen's visions wait the midnight hour:
The mystick treasure, plac'd beneath her head,
Will tell the fair – if haply she may wed.

This ancient tradition of passing tiny pieces of the cake nine times through a wedding ring in imitation of the act of coitus survived well into the nineteenth century.[7]

If the bride cake was originally a part of the religious rites associated with the wedding procession, a remarkable pie may once have been the chief attraction of the feast, apparently offering entertainment as well as sustenance. In his *Accomplisht Cook*, first published in 1660, Robert May gives a recipe for a bride pie, a kaleidoscopic assemblage of shaped pies which together form a pastry knot garden, roughly in the shape of a Tudor rose (see figs 7 & 8). Each pie has its own filling. Some contain alleged aphrodisiacs, such as cock's stones, cock's combs and oysters, while the central pie is hollow and filled with 'live birds, or a snake, which will seem strange to the beholders, which cut up the pie at the Table. This is only for a Wedding to pass the time of day.'[8]

From the seventeenth to the nineteenth centuries the benediction posset – a blend of eggs, cream and sack or ale – was used to toast the bride and groom

FIG. 9
Stanhope Alexander Forbes (1857–1947), *The Health of the Bride*, 1889
Oil on canvas, 152.4 × 200 cm

Newlyn in the 1880s, with its luminous light and bracing freshness, was the ideal spot for the ambitious young artist Stanhope Forbes to pursue his ideal of painting everyday scenes in the open, away from the stifling academic conventions and synthetic sentimentality of contemporary studio work. But it took some strength of character to endure the bleak curiosity of the locals, not to mention the boisterous weather and equally boisterous small children on beach and street.

Sometimes he felt the need to retreat to the studio, and it was there that he assembled friends and acquaintances to pose as participants in this typical small-town scene, with the local inn as background. The pleasant atmosphere of the scene relies on an understated realism in which personalities and details of clothing, furnishings and vestiges of food and drink all contribute to the impression of a natural, unpretentious occasion.

The girl posing as the bride could not have known how close the conventional details of her simulated wedding were to the more grandiose ceremony in Bermondsey four centuries earlier. Her posy and wreath contain the same symbolic blossoms and her hair is free of the obligatory bonnets and hats of the guests. Before her the wedding cake sits in splendour, finished with the almond paste and sugar coating of tradition, but, as can be seen from the slices on the plates, it is a darker, richer confection than the ancient yeasted dough of the sixteenth-century bride cake. The local Newlyn baker may well have followed the recipe in the first edition of Mrs Beeton's *Book of Household Management*, which produces a monster weighing in at over a stone, costed at two shillings a pound.[9] It was made with a rich mix of dried fruit, spices, butter, eggs and the finest flour – an expensive prop for an impoverished young painter, which perhaps accounts for the small size of the cake in the painting, probably consisting of half quantities. The Manchester confectioner Elizabeth Raffald in 1769 published the earliest recipe for a bride cake of this kind.[10] Paler than a modern wedding cake, it was made with a smaller proportion of currants to candied citron and was coated with an icing subtly perfumed with rosewater.

before they retired to the nuptial bed. This intoxicating nightcap consisted of a frothy head of aerated custard floating on a draught of highly alcoholic liquor. The custard was eaten with a spoon, while the liquid was sucked piping hot through the spout of the posset pot. As a wedding night pick-me-up, it had universal appeal and was consumed by all classes with a great deal of elbow-nudging and mirth.

The humble farmers of northern England drank ale posset at their daughters' weddings from slipware spoutpots passed around the company and then given to the couple as a souvenir of the happy occasion. Many that have survived bear a double monogram showing both the bride's and the groom's initials. The nobility and gentry were able to afford more refined silver vessels, or delftware pots from the Lambeth or Bristol factories (fig. 10; see also fig. 30). At an important society wedding at Belvoir in 1693 huge quantities of sack posset were served from an enormous silver cistern or wine-cooler:

> *After supper, which was exceeding magnificent, the whole company went in procession to the great hall; the bride and bridegroom first, and all the rest in order, two and two; there it was the scene opened, and the great cistern appeared, and the healths began; first in spoons some time after in silver cups; and tho' the healths were many, and great variety of names were given to them, it was observed after one hour's hot service, the posset did not sink above one inch.*[11]

Other important rites of passage were also honoured with special foods. Women 'in travail' entertained visitors to the birth chamber, again with the ubiquitous comfits. 'A note of the spices at the tyme of my Mistress lyinge in child bedd', from 12 September 1617, lists ten kinds, including coriander, orris, violet, rosemary and ambergris.[12] Funeral feasts or arvels were also important: 'On the decease of any person possessed of valuable effects, the friends and neighbours of the Family are invited to dinner on the Day of Interment, which is called the Arthel or Arvel-dinner.'[13] At Lakeland funerals wiggs (arvel bread, in the form of small buns flavoured with caraway seeds and other spices) were distributed to the guests. In other parts of the country funeral biscuits of the sponge finger variety were distributed among the mourners. These, too, were usually spiced with seeds, a universal symbol of resurrection and renewed life, and often wrapped in crêpe paper edged with black.

FIG. 10
English delftware posset pots and sack bottles

Sack, a strong white Spanish wine, was a popular ingredient in posset, which were traditionally served piping hot. Since a certain time was needed for the custard to separate out from the alcoholic whey, the posset needed to be rested, usually close to the fire. One seventeenth-century manuscript receipt book instructs us to surround the pot with cushions in order to prevent the posset from cooling too much. Tin-glazed earthenware has been called delftware in Britain since the eighteenth century. The earliest was made in London and Norwich, but by the late seventeenth century manufactories had been established in Bristol, Brislington and Belfast. In the eighteenth century the technique spread to Wincanton, Glasgow, Dublin and Liverpool.

LEFT TO RIGHT:

Sack bottle (small), London, dated in underglaze blue 1650.

Posset pot (large), decorated in underglaze blue with scrolling foliage and dots, probably Bristol or Brislington, 1710–30.

Posset pot (small), decorated in underglaze blue with foliage and dated 1669 with initials SW.

Sack bottle (large), either London or (possibly) Norwich, dated in underglaze blue 1649 with initials EMW around the arms of the Grocers' Company. The initials may be those of E. M. Woodyard, a Norwich grocer known to have issued a farthing token in 1656.

SACK
1650

FIG. 11
William Powell Frith (1819–1909), *Many Happy Returns of the Day*, 1856
Oil on canvas, 101.8 × 134.8 cm

Although this painting, celebrating the birthday of Frith's little daughter Alice, shows various members of the family (with a professional model posing for the grandfather), it is unlikely to be a group portrait. It is, in fact, more an overview of contemporary ideas of domestic felicity – the women emerging from their indoor realm to offer presents, admire dotingly and oversee the birthday party, while the men, cool amidst all the fun, sit close to the window and the wide world beyond, remaining aloof from the unrestrained tippling of the small boys.

There is, nonetheless, a premonition of tears before bedtime, which Ruskin characteristically picked up: 'One is only sorry to see any fair little child having too many and too kind friends, and in so great danger of being toasted, toyed and wreathed into selfishness and misery.'[14] Frith himself wrote about the work in his autobiography (1887). On the subject of the little girl, he remarks: 'The heroine sits in a high chair, which has been decorated for the occasion with a wreath of flowers, and is somewhat bewildered by the uproarious brothers and sisters, whose wishes for many happy returns of the day are screamed by half a dozen shrill voices.'[15]

Indeed, the wreath, cake and riotous fun place this work in the tradition of Netherlandish genre scenes, where rites of passage are more significant than individual portraiture and traditional food and drink play their part in reinforcing social conventions and legitimizing excesses of gluttony and merriment.

Children's birthday parties do not seem to have become a feature of English family life until the reign of Victoria, nor do they seem to have changed very much since. Frith's painting of his daughter Alice's party (fig. 11) includes a cake very similar to so many of those lovingly baked today. Many regional foods associated with calendar events sadly vanished with social changes brought about by the industrial revolution and the coming of the railways. One victim of these dramatic changes was the long-forgotten Christmas dish of plum pottage, a spicy, sweet-and-sour broth thickened with currants and generously fortified with canary wine and port.[16]

National rites of passage such as victories and coronations have always been celebrated with great feasts. While ordinary folk caroused on the village greens or in the streets, the great and the good rejoiced at tables glittering with plate laden with the most fashionable luxury foods. One such occasion was the remarkable Allied Banquet of 1814, held in the London Guildhall to celebrate victory over Napoleon. The style of both the food and the table decorations depicted in Luke Clennel's painting of this event (fig. 12) illustrates how celebrations in the City had moved on from the time of Moufet and Hake. The herons and swans had given way to a highly developed Anglo-French cuisine, though some ancient customs such as distributing the leftovers to the poor did survive (see fig. 13).

However, the great social upheavals of the decades following Waterloo meant that, for some, these token displays of largesse were not enough to relieve the problems caused by growing urban deprivation. In 1830 the cancellation of a banquet planned for the instalment of Lord Mayor John Key created a political scandal. In an open letter to the King, highly critical of the waste and expense, one commentator wrote: 'We think it rather a fearful omen that your majesty did not at once check the pompous propensity to profligacy in the expenditure of the citizens' money by this little junta, this City Parliament.'[17] The political cartoonists of the day savagely lampooned the unfortunate Key by portraying him as a donkey (Don Key). One satirical print shows him being tormented in his dreams by an intimidating Fuselian turtle sitting heavily on his chest (fig. 14).

Of all the great national celebration feasts, perhaps coronation dinners have always been the most magnificent and therefore usually the best recorded. In order to ensure the continuity of the ancient customs associated with the coronation after the upheavals of the Civil War and Commonwealth, a detailed account of the coronation of James II was published by Francis Sandford in

1687.[18] His description of James's great feast in Westminster Hall includes a table plan (fig. 15). It is interesting to note that foods considered humble today, such as 'hog's feet' and 'periwinkles cold', were happily distributed among delicacies like 'botargo' (preserved mullet's roe), 'mangoes' and 'venison pasties hot'.

Although it includes many lingering elements of medieval ceremonial and gastronomy, the 1671 Garter feast described in the following essay illustrates the magnificence of English baroque entertainments of this kind. Upstaged only by the great coronation feasts of the period, this annual celebration meal of the

FIG. 12
Luke Clennell (1781–1840), *Banquet given by the Corporation of London to the Prince Regent, the Emperor of Russia and the King of Prussia, June 18th, 1814*
Oil on canvas, 127 × 190.5 cm

The banquet laid on by the Corporation of London for the Allied Heads of State on 18 June 1814 was a triumph of last-minute organization as well as a celebration of the defeat of Napoleon. Once the Entertainment Committee of the Court of Common Council had authorized the meal and the Prince Regent had graciously accepted their invitation, the city fathers had only eight days in which to arrange an entertainment of a magnificence appropriate to the occasion. The food seems to have been the least of their worries; not only decorations, but structural alterations and a billowing tide of carpets, drapes, hangings, chandeliers, lustres and gold and silver plate surged into the extended and refurbished Guildhall at a total expense of £20,038.7s.10d.

The royal table was 'most sumptuous in its display of gold plate; its richness indeed was unparalleled: magnificent ornaments ... candelabra, epergnes, tureens, ewers, cups, dishes, glaciers, &c being selected for the purpose; and the great body of light from thereon, produced a most striking and brilliant effect'. Clennell's painting shows the dessert course, where the hothouse fruit could hardly compete with the glitter of the plate, partly the Guildhall's own, some borrowed from City companies and private individuals and the rest hired for the sum of £1,120.7s.9d. The Bill of Fare does not survive, but the sum of £2,899.18s.9d was paid to the cooks, Messrs Birch & Angell, and the confectioners, Messrs Hoffmans, and the tidy sum of £18 to Mr Edward Hanson for oranges. Altogether the food, wines, butlerage and associated expenses came to £5,337.18s.0d, more than a quarter of the total cost, even allowing for the convenience of recycling the remaining wines at a party given a few weeks later for the Duke of Wellington.

Clennell certainly captured the glitter of the occasion, with a frenzied, rapid technique that may reveal something of the mental turmoil into which the task plunged him. For the public triumph was to become a private tragedy for the artist. The strain of executing Lord Bridgewater's commission to produce a grand painting of the occasion pushed an already distraught personality into permanent insanity.[19]

FIG. 13
Adrien-Emmanuel Marie (1848–91),
Distributing Left-overs to the Poor after the Lord Mayor's Banquet at the Guildhall, 1882
Oil on canvas, 92 × 132 cm

Distributing the remains of a grand banquet to the poor was part of a long tradition of largesse, a benign way of counterbalancing the overproduction of banquet dishes that characterized noble and corporate feasting. During the late medieval period it was customary for the leftovers of a royal feast to be collected in baskets by the household almoner and shared out among the needy. Those from the 1882 Lord Mayor's Banquet were handed formally to the fortunate recipients of tickets issued by members of the Lord Mayor and Sheriff's committee. A hundred and twenty tickets were printed. A report in a contemporary newspaper relates: 'The remains consisted of turkeys,

fowl, duck, geese, tongues, joints of beef and mutton pies, and other viands, many of which had not been cut. The lots, which were as far as possible made of equal size, and generally about as much as one person could conveniently carry, were quite enough to supply the wants of a moderately numerous family for at least a week.'

Fig. 14
Lithograph by MG, *Fatal Effects of Gluttony – A Lord Mayor's Day Night Mare*, published by Thomas McLean (1788–1875), 1830
Dimensions: 25 x 35 cm

In this satirical print, based loosely on Henry Fuseli's *Nightmare*, the unfortunate John Key dreams of his phantom Lord Mayor's banquet of 1830, which was cancelled at the last minute (see p.25). Wielding two champagne bottles like pistols, he attempts to ward off the assaults of the animals that would have been served at the feast. A lobster pinching his nose leads the sortie, while a grinning sturgeon in the background prepares to join the second wave of the attack. Gleefully rotating frogs impaled on a spit, an incubus in the form of a diabolical turnspit is urged on by the other vengeful birds and beasts. It would seem that the Lord Mayor had read the bill of fare of the abortive banquet just before he fell asleep, as it sits abandoned among the surfeit water and other digestive medicines on his bedside table.

Knights of the Garter was brought to table with all the pomp and theatricality essential to courtly dining in the seventeenth century. Recipes for most of the dishes can readily be found in contemporary cookery books, especially those of Robert May and William Rabisha. Although the meal consisted chiefly of an extraordinary array of luxury foods, including wild boar pie, Lucca olives and baked buck, not all were exclusively aristocratic. Mutton marinated in blood, and haggis, for example, had been enjoyed for generations at less privileged tables. Alongside ancient court dishes of late medieval and Tudor origin, like the sweet chicken pie with its old-fashioned sugar-frosted crust, ice cream makes its first recorded appearance at a British meal, albeit that it was served

FIG. 15
The table plan for the King's table at the coronation feast of James II, an illustration from Francis Sandford's *History of the Coronation of James II* (London 1687). Items 69, 73 and 77 are complex pyramids of sweetmeats.This remarkable dinner was created by the King's master cook Patrick Lamb, who also prepared John Holles' instalment feast at Windsor in 1698 (see fig. 23).

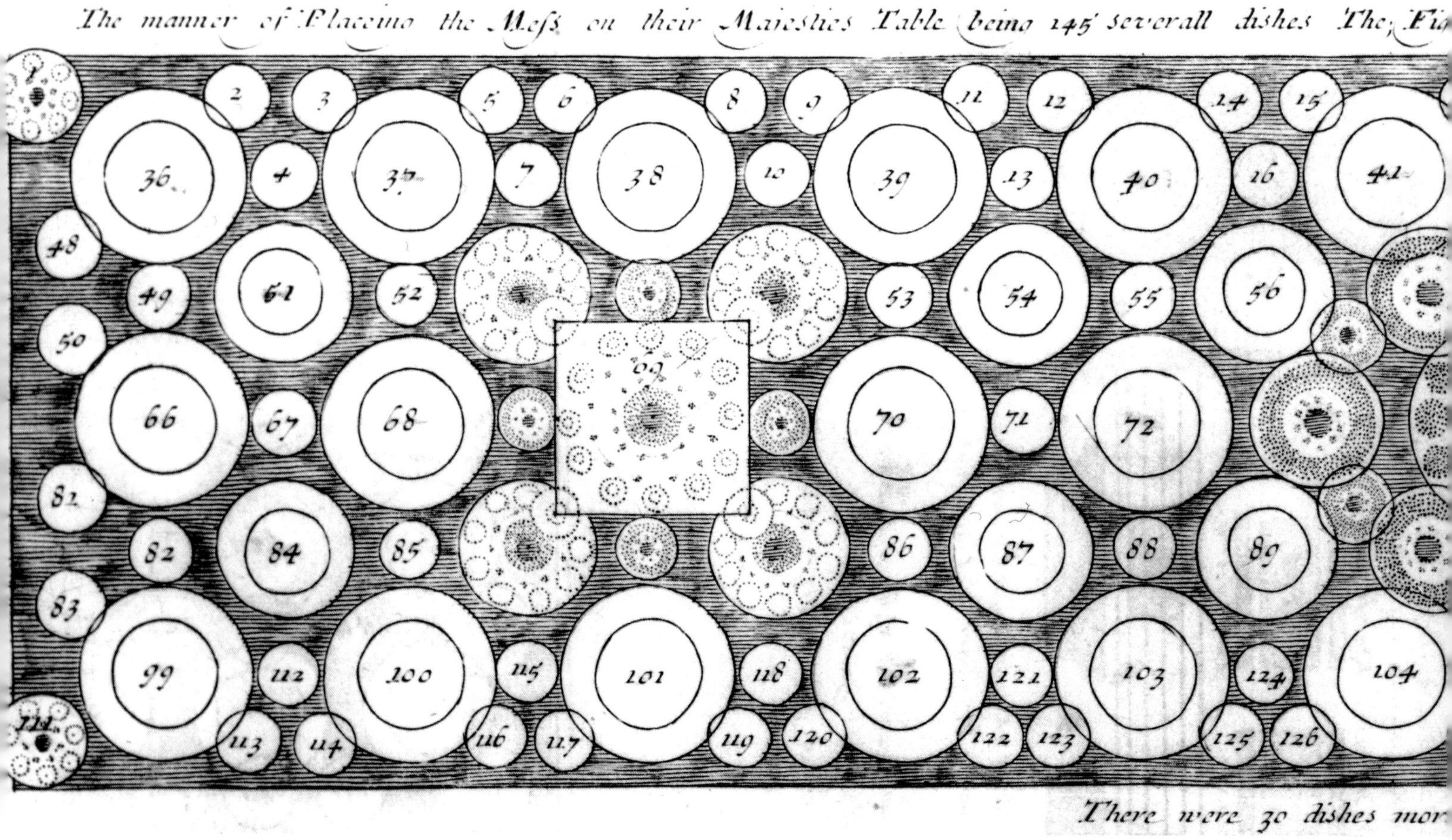

only at the King's table. The influence of the new French court cuisine was not yet as significant as it was to be in John Holles' instalment feast served at Windsor twenty-seven years later (see figs 3, 22 & 23), when the meal opened with a selection of richly seasoned bisques and pottages.

From a modern-day perspective, the complex and ancient ceremonial that accompanied this extraordinary meal appears mannered and ostentatious. But at a time when the aristocracy were re-establishing and consolidating their power, the King's subjects would have seen this display of ancient and solemn rites as proof of the continuity and permanence of the crown and its traditions.

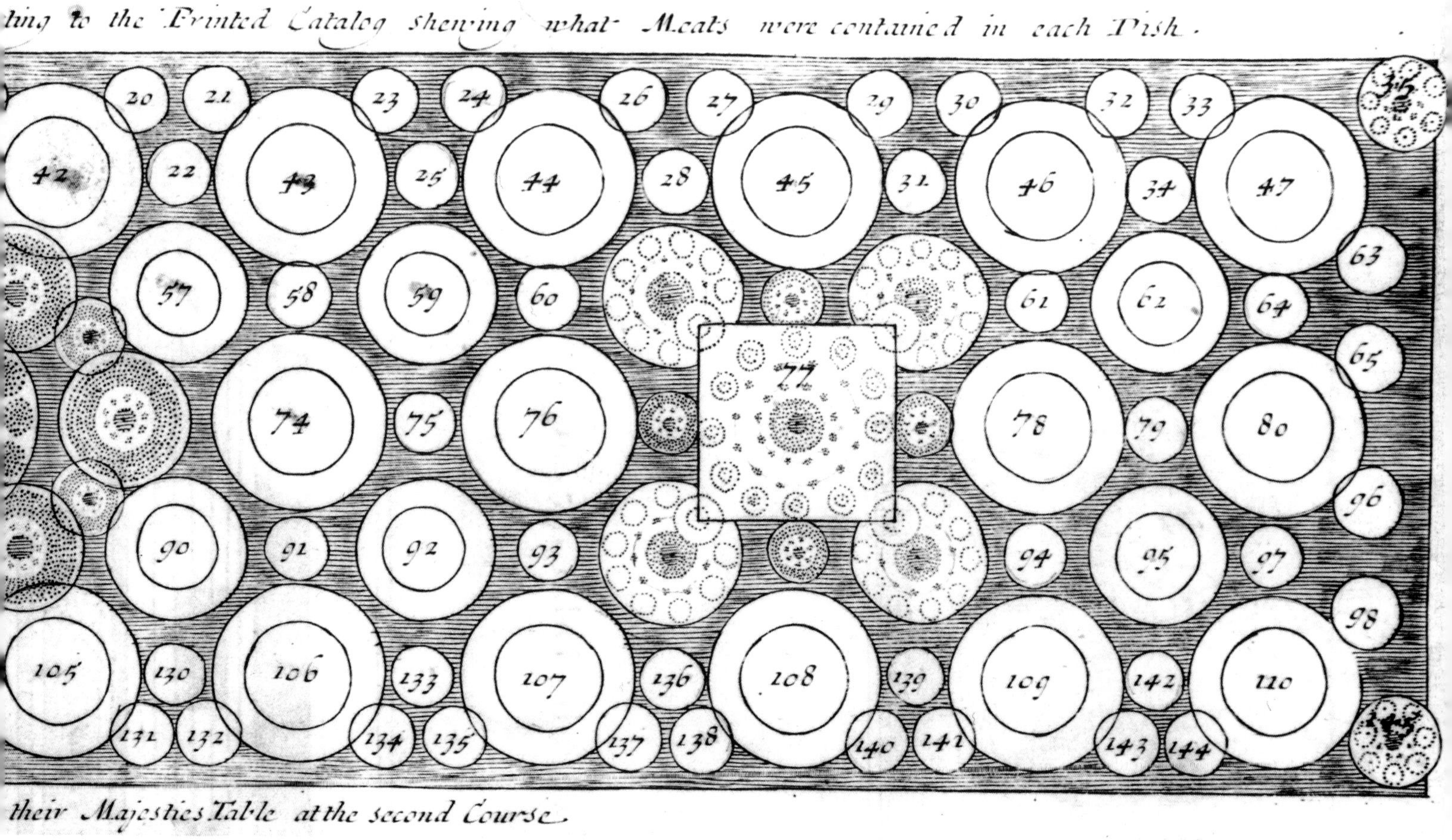

Fig. 16
Wenceslaus Hollar (1607–77), *The Prospect of the Inside of St George's Hall, Windsor*, detail from an illustration in Elias Ashmole's *Institution, Laws and Ceremonies of the Most Noble Order of the Garter* (London 1672)

This detail of the Knight's table shows how the rims of plates were garnished. The complex stews of the first course, so popular at court at this time, were garnished with small bone-marrow pies called chewitts. Garnishes for plate rims included cock's combs, truffles, olives, capers, 'jagged' citrus slices and 'jagged' beetroot. The crowded profusion of dishes on the table is similar to the arrangements represented in Houkgeest's painting of Charles I dining at Whitehall (fig. 34) and James II's coronation dinner (figs 15 and 33). It is no wonder that the English aristocracy attempted to alleviate their troubled digestion with surfeit waters, medicinal comfits and soothing marmalades. Note the larded fowls in the foreground.

The Garter Feast of 1671

EVER since its foundation by Edward III in 1348, Europe's senior order of chivalry, the Sovereign and Knights of the most noble Order of the Garter, has celebrated its great annual feast each spring with religious services, chapter meetings and formal meals of extreme grandeur. Throughout their six-hundred-and-fifty years both the ceremonies and the menus of the Garter feasts have slowly progressed through gradual adaptation to changing social conventions and gastronomic tastes.

In the later seventeenth century a number of major historical reviews of state ceremonies were undertaken by members of the College of Arms in order to provide a solid foundation for planning both present and future events. It is extremely rare to find any historical meal described in quite the detail with which Elias Ashmole (1617–92) diligently recorded for posterity the full magnificence of a Garter feast. This feast, in which Ashmole, as a herald, had only recently participated, is comprehensively described and illustrated in his *Institution, Laws and Ceremonies of the Most Noble Order of the Garter* of 1672 (see illustration detail opposite).[20] Having witnessed the Commonwealth's disruption of English court life, Ashmole must have been particularly aware of the importance of his work in the restoration of major ceremonies; some three hundred years later his evidence is still of immense value to historians working in many disciplines. Ashmole's contemporary, Francis Sandford, Lancaster Herald, also gathered together everything 'that might preserve the Memory of this Glorious Solemnity, in all its Incidents and Circumstances, so nothing has been so much Endeavour'd, as to Render it truly Useful to Posterity'.[21]

Ashmole's book includes much detail of the various Garter feasts, but we deal here with a single event, the dinner served at the Garter feast held in St George's Hall at Windsor Castle on Monday, 28 May 1671. This is a truly remarkable meal, one that still retained, in its rituals and recipes, much of the scale and grandeur of high medieval ceremonial feasts. For instance, the various officers who attended on the sovereign at table performed duties that had changed little since the fifteenth century, when they had been codified in books of manners and carving such as Wynken de Worde's *Boke of Kervynge*.[22]

By the morning of the previous day preparations were already well advanced in the castle kitchen, a vast room still in use today, lined with roasting hearths and lit by high rows of clerestory windows. Here the Clerk of the Kitchen and his staff had assembled a mountain of fine food, including huge amounts of beef, mutton, lamb, pork and bacon, 2,158 head of poultry, 410 rabbits, 136 lobsters, 1,500 crayfish, 16 barrels of pickled oysters, 6,000 asparagus, 200 artichokes, 370 lbs of butter, 2,000 eggs, and other delicacies such as cock's combs and stones, lamb's stones, Westphalia hams, sturgeon, caviar and anchovies, not to mention the indispensable 24 sheep's feet and 24 calves' feet for making jellies, the small gut of an ox for encasing the almond puddings, and the haggis bags for that most English of puddings, the haggis, a delectable mixture of minced offal, oatmeal and onions encased in a sheep's paunch.

Meanwhile, in the Pastry the staff were busy making over 140 hot pies of venison, steak, chicken, umbles (the intestines of venison), eggs and cream and 90 cold pies of wild boar, red deer, tongue, capon and lampreys. The total cost of the raw materials alone came to £2,394.17s.8½d in 1671. In addition, the royal Confectionery brought in 234 lbs of dry confections. Although not itemized, these would have included the customary array of sugar-coated seeds,

FIG. 17
Joseph Highmore (1692–1780),
The Knights of the Order of the Bath at Dinner – Prince William at the bringing of the second course, *c.*1750
Etching (detail)

Highmore's print shows 'the Knights at dinner, Bath King of Arms proclaiming the style of Prince William ... attended by Heralds and Pursuivants'. Note the pyramids of salvers with jellies or syllabub for the banquet that follows the second course. Pyramids of fruit and sweetmeats were also arranged on tiers of salvers, though they were becoming a little old fashioned by the middle of the eighteenth century.

spices and nuts habitually consumed after a surfeit of rich foods in order to aid digestion. By now, earlier fears about 'fluxes' caused by the consumption of fresh fruit were being overcome, as witness the 48 pounds of Duke cherries, 22 gallons of strawberries and, exclusively for the King's table, 50 China oranges. The latter were a recently introduced novelty whose sweet flesh could be eaten with relish, unlike the more commonly available bitter oranges whose sour juice and peel had provided an important flavouring and garnish in English court kitchens since the end of the thirteenth century. The most luxurious item of the banquet course was the ice cream served at the King's table.[23]

The Bakehouse would have provided the manchet loaves of fine bread, the coarser 'cheat' loaves and the really coarse bread (see p.70), and the Buttery the ale, beer, French wines and sack, so that the total cost must have been in the order of £3,000 for materials alone, with the remainder of the staff, napery, tableware costs and so forth all being absorbed by the Royal Household.

On the feast day itself, after taking breakfast and attending morning service in the chapel the Sovereign and the Knights retired to the Privy Lodgings while St George's Hall was prepared for the dinner, the Sovereign's table being set up beneath the long canopy of state, on the raised dais railed off at the upper end of the hall. Along the body of the hall a row of court cupboards was set up beneath the windows, each having the ewer, basin, towel, plates, beakers and everything else required to serve each pair of Knights. Their seats were arranged against the opposite wall, with a row of dining tables before them – seven tables being set up for this particular feast, since some fourteen Knights were in attendance. The ceremony began with the King's Musick sounding their wind instruments from the gallery as the Sovereign's first course (see Bill of Fare, pp.36–7) was borne solemnly in by a procession consisting of, among other officers, two Sergeants at Arms, the Sewer and twenty Gentlemen Pensioners, and finally the Master of Household followed by the Clerks of the Kitchen and his staff.

On reaching the Sovereign's table, starting at the southern end the Sewer set out the first fourteen dishes as seven pairs down its length; he then mounted the remaining dishes on stands between the pairs down the centre.

Having been informed that his first course was on the table, the Sovereign, led by the Officers of the Garter and followed by the Knights, proceeded to the Presence Chamber. Here he stood beneath the canopy of state while the Knights arranged themselves in the order of their installation, the junior knights to the front, before bowing to the Sovereign, who returned their salutation. Then, led by pairs of Alms-Knights, Prebends and Officers of Arms and followed by the Officers of the Garter, they preceded the Sovereign through the Guardroom and into St George's Hall. Here the Alms-Knights fell off to their right, followed in turn by the Prebends and then the Officers of Arms, of whom Clarenceaux (the second King-of-Arms in England), heading this line, stood a few yards below the dais. The Knights then fell off in a similar manner to their left, against their respective dining tables, with the senior Knights closest to the dais. Once this processional avenue had been formed, the Officers of the Garter led the Sovereign up the hall.

While still standing before his table, the Sovereign was approached with three bows by the Lord Chamberlain, leading a group of noblemen bearing the ewer, basin and towel for the ceremonial washing of hands in perfumed water. In medieval times this was a practical necessity throughout the meal, when the elegantly carved and presented food was conveyed to the mouth between first finger and thumb, or on the point of a knife.

After this group had retired, the Prelate said grace and the Sovereign took his seat at the table beneath the canopy of state, facing down the hall. At this point the Knights replaced their caps (having removed them for grace) and moved towards their tables, where two gentlemen of quality brought a ewer, basin and towel to each pair so that they, too, could wash. The Senior Knights then walked from their place near the dais, down the hall before the open side of their tables then back up the wall side, followed by the other Knights, until each reached his seat – two sitting behind each table, in order of seniority.

At this point their first course was brought to them by the Yeomen of the Guard and served by some of the Gentlemen Pensioners and other royal servants. The course was served as a single mess to each of the seven tables:

Wild boar pie   Chine of beef
12 boiled ducklings   Stump pie   8 fried rabbits
Gammon of bacon   Shoulder of mutton & 4 great pullets in blood, & steaks
3 great carps   Salads of pickles
12 boiled chickens   Baked Buck   4 fat capons

Once this had been served, a 'press of People ... thronged towards the Knights-Companions' Tables, out of Curiosity to behold them sit at Dinner and observe their Services.' When the second course was about to be served this crowd was removed to the window side of the hall, so that the Sovereign could see all his Knights. The Knights then rose, removed their caps while the King drank to

Bill of Fare

(A MODERN TRANSCRIPTION)

The King's first course

1. *Wild boar pie*
2. *Salmon*
3. *Chine of beef*
4. *Haggis pudding*
5. *Batalia pie & patties*
6. *Gammon & 12 tame pigeons*
7. *12 boiled ducklings*
8. *12 boiled chickens*
9. *6 chines mutton & veal*
10. *2 roasted pikes*
11. *Baked buck*
12. *6 green geese*
13. *3 great carps*
14. *Frosted chicken pie*
15. *Salad*
16. *Sweetbreads*
17. *Almond puddings*
18. *Petty patties*
19. *Hashed salad*
20. *Chickens marinaded 4 capons*

The King's second course

1. *6 soused pullets*
2. *Tongue pies*
3. *12 roast rabbits*
4. *Cream tarts*

5. 6 pheasants with eggs
6. 6 buttered crabs
7. 24 quails
8. 12 tame pigeons
9. 6 lobsters
10. 12 fat chickens
11. Gammon bacon &
12. 12 ruffs ... 2 tongues
13. Sorts of tarts
14. 12 ducklings
15. Salads of pickles
16. Eggs of Portugal
17. Jelly
18. Luke [Lucca] *olives*
19. Peas
20. Prawns

The King's banquet course

1 charger of 50 China oranges
7 chargers each with 20 1-lb boxes of dry confections
2 plates, each with 4 lbs of Duke cherries
1 plate with 1 gallon of red strawberries
1 plate with 2 gallons of white strawberries
1 plate of ice cream
3 plates, each with 3 lbs of liquid sweetmeats

them, then drank to him, replaced their caps, and sat down once more. Garter (the principal King of Arms) then loudly cried 'Largess! Largess! Largess!', all the Knights (except kings and great princes) then standing bareheaded. He then proclaimed the Sovereign's styles and titles of honour, first in Latin, then in French and English – 'Of the most High, Most Excellent, and most mighty Monarch, Charles the Second, by the Grace of God King of Great Britain, France and Ireland, Defender of the Faith, and Sovereign of the most Noble Order of the Garter!' – all the Officers of Arms bowing at the end of each proclamation, and crying 'Largess!' three times after the English version. The Treasurer of the Household then placed the Sovereign's largess of £10 in gold into Garter's hat, this sum later being divided among the Officers of Arms, according to custom.

Now with caps in their hand the fully robed officers processed into the hall with the Sovereign's second course. The Sewer arranged these dishes in the same manner as the first course, and then the Yeomen of the Guard brought the Knights' second course:

4 Pheasants 18 quails
Artichokes Anchovies, caviar & pickled oysters
12 fat chickens Sorts of tarts
6 ducklings & 6 green geese Lamprey pie Jelly
Gamon bacon & 2 tongues 12 tame pigeons Red deer pie

The Sovereign's banquet or dessert course was brought in with the identical procession to that described above, except that the Clerk of the Kitchen was replaced by the Chief Clerk of the Spicery.

The Yeomen of the Guard then brought in the Knights' banquet of seven messes of:

2 chargers, each with 14 1-lb boxes of dry confections
1 plate of 2 lbs of Duke cherries
1 plate of 1 gallon of red strawberries
1 plate of 3 lbs liquid sweetmeats

When the banquet finally came to an end, the Knights rose, washed their hands as before, then assembled in pairs. After the Prelate had said grace, the Lord Chamberlain led forward the group of nobles bearing the Sovereign's ewer, basin and towel, so that he too could wash. Once this ceremony had been completed, the Sovereign took off his cap, bowed to the Knights and left the hall.

The Duke of Newcastle's Feast

FIGS 18 & 19
Designs for lobster and salmon pies used as illustrations in Robert May's *The Accomplisht Cook* (London 1660), which contains many woodcuts. Though these are crudely executed they give us a clear idea of the appearance of the highly decorative food of the seventeenth century. Some of May's designs may have come from continental sources. An unusual fiddle-shaped hare pie which he illustrates also appears in a number of seventeenth century Antwerp school still life paintings.

TO ILLUSTRATE the court style of dining described in the previous essay, we have re-created a later Garter instalment feast, served at Windsor in 1698, from an illustration in Patrick Lamb's book *Royal Cookery* of 1710 (fig. 23). Lamb is described as 'Near Fifty Years Master-Cook to their late Majesties King Charles II, King James II, King William and Queen Mary and Queen Anne'. His impressive culinary career started in 1662 as a child apprentice in the Pastry of the royal kitchens. By 1677 he had risen to the rank of master cook to the Queen and by 1684 he was master cook to Charles II. The apogee of Lamb's career was the preparation of the Coronation Feast for James II in Westminster Hall in April 1685. However, the new King was anxious to keep up with the latest gastronomic fashions spreading from the court at Versailles and in July 1685 he decided to employ the Frenchman Claude Fourment as master cook. Lamb was demoted to the post of second master cook and yeoman of the Pastry. He regained his former position under both William III and Queen Anne, and superintended the royal kitchens until his death in 1709.

Unfortunately, Lamb's plate of Newcastle's feast is not dated, but it is almost certainly a table plan of the Garter instalment feast of John Holles (1662–1711), eldest son of the 3rd Earl of Clare. Holles, a prominent Whig, played an active role in the Glorious Revolution and was rewarded for his services to the Protestant cause by being appointed gentleman of the bedchamber to William III in 1689. Five years later he was made Duke of Newcastle and on 30 May 1698 he was conferred to the Order of the Garter. Important feasts such as Garter instalment dinners are usually recorded in the royal warrant books under 'Diets, extraordinary', but unfortunately the entries for 1698 have not survived so the only documentary evidence that this meal ever took place is the plate in Lamb's *Royal Cookery*; figs 3 & 22 illustrate a re-creation of the second course of Holles' feast.

This kind of table arrangement, where the dessert was presented on the table at the same time as the dishes of the first and second courses, was known

FIGS 20 & 21
Re-creations of lobster and salmon pies from May's designs. The lobster pie is garnished with 'jagged' lemons and Luke (Lucca) olives, while the salmon pie is surrounded with oyster chewitts. Pies of this kind were constructed from a 'standing crust' made by mixing boiling water and butter into the flour. Once cold, this stiff gluten-rich pastry was ideal for raising these complex structures, though it did not make for particularly good eating.

as an ambigue, a style of dining popularized by French court protocol. The first course opened with the *grosses entrées*. Lamb and his kitchen staff would have started preparations for these richly flavoured pottages and bisques of fowl, duckling and pigeons very early in the morning. Once they had been served and the tureens (usually spelt 'terrines' at this time) removed from the table, the four vacant spaces were filled with the removes, the supplementary dishes of the first course – in this case, a roasted salmon and made dishes of turbot, carp and chicken. The principal dishes were large joints of venison, mutton and pig, as well as lamb marinated in its own blood. One contemporary recipe, 'To roast a shoulder of mutton in blood', instructs us to cut holes in the flesh and fill them with blood, as well as a forcemeat of onions, savory and sweet marjoram. The joint was then wrapped in caul and allowed to soak in its marinade of blood for a day before being roasted at the fire. The purpose of the process was to create a darker meat with a richer, gamier flavour. All the large joints would have been rotated on spits at the great roasting range in the hours leading up to the meal and presented to table piping hot. Guests could also choose at the first course from a large selection of pies arranged in a stack and a pulpatoon, a dish of pigeons dressed in a rich ragoo and baked in a forcemeat crust.

The feast continued with a second course of elaborate pies of wild boar and lobster that had been prepared earlier in the Pastry. The designs used here are from Robert May's *Accomplisht Cook* (1660) and Edward Kidder's *Receipts in Pastry and Cookery* (1720), the two most important illustrated cookery texts of the period (see figs 18–21 & 24–6). However, the chief dishes of the second course were roasted fowl and game, freshly prepared at the roasting range while the guests were feasting on the elaborate dishes of the first course. Each animal or bird would have been trussed using the method customary for that particular creature. Leverets were prepared with their heads (complete with ears) looking back over their shoulders and with one side larded, so that the diners had a choice of larded or unlarded meat. Rabbits were roasted *sans* ears and with their heads pointing forward. Chickens, pheasants and quail were roasted with heads and legs intact, while aquatic birds such as ducks and geese were prepared without the head. The rims of dishes were frequently garnished with small tid-bits, such as cock's combs, truffles, morels, slices of lemon, olives and capers (see figs 20 & 24). When the guests had eaten their fill of the first- and second-course dishes, they completed the meal by consuming the fruit and sweetmeats of the banquet from the tall pyramids erected on tiers of salvers.

Fig. 22
Aerial view of the Duke of Newcastle's Feast re-created in the great baroque hall of Castle Howard, Yorkshire, after the table plan – reproduced on the right – in Patrick Lamb's *Royal Cookery* (London 1710)

The central pyramid consists of a tier of three salvers covered in an array of typical sweetmeats of the period. These include ragged long comfits, wafers, bane bread and candies of green oranges, green almonds, eryngo roots and gillyflowers in Spanish wedges.

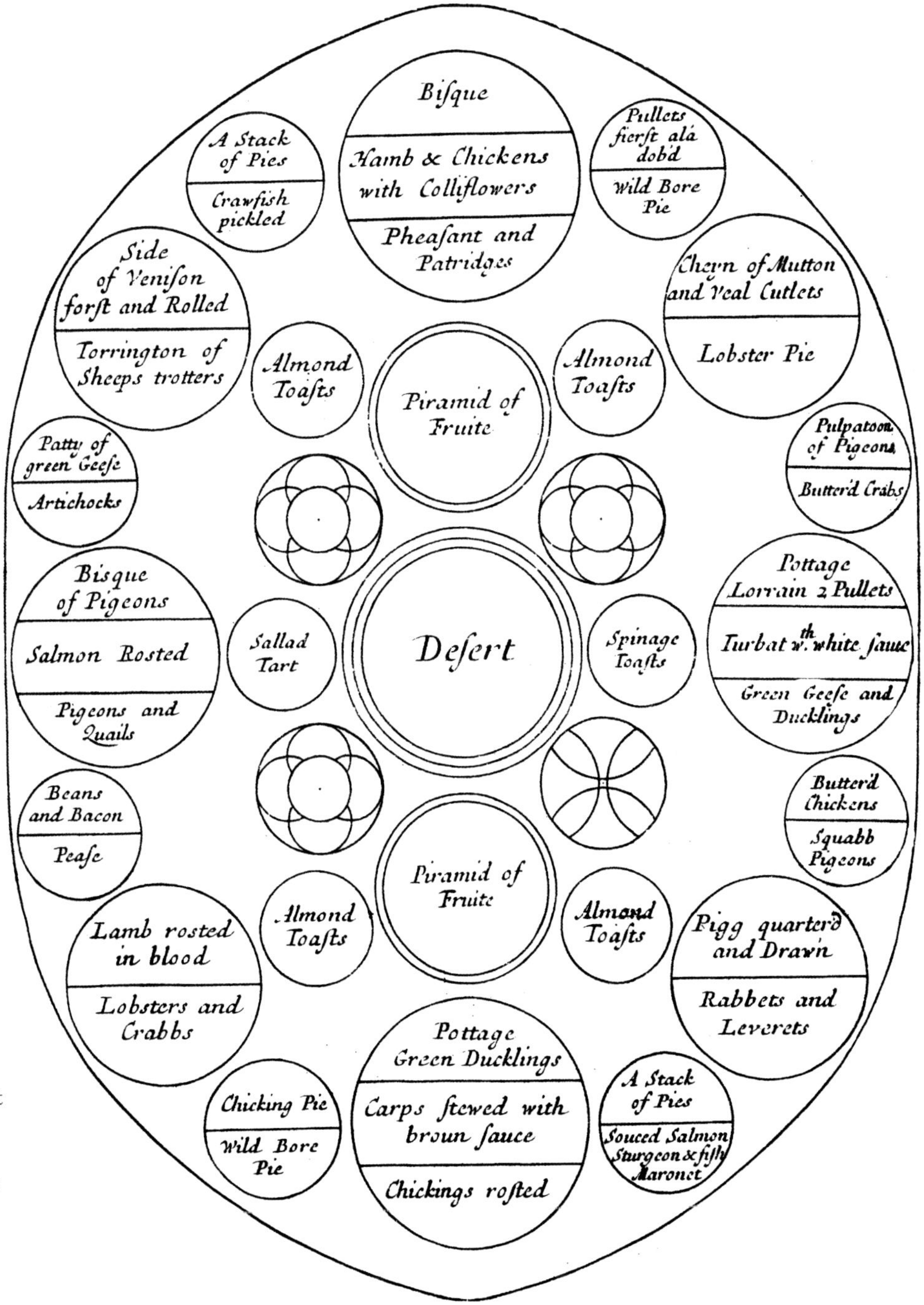

Fig. 23
Table plan of the Duke of Newcastle's Feast at Windsor, from Lamb's book cited above

The lower division of each plate represents an item of the second course. It is these second-course foods that appear on the table opposite.

FIG. 24
Shaped mince pies based on a design from Edward Kidder's *Pastry and Cookery* (London n.d., *c.*1720)

These pies were arranged in the same symmetrical style as the more complex bride pies, a baroque fashion that appears to have survived until the middle of the eighteenth century. The rim of the plate is garnished with almond comfits.

Lamb's table plan is vague when it comes to specifying the type of equipage in use on the table. It is not clear, for example, whether the tiers of salvers were made of metal or of the recently developed 'flint' glass. Stands made of glass were certainly available at this time, although perhaps not to the large diameter indicated in the layout. Early references suggest that these stands were usually associated with 'crewetts' and it is possible that the four curious structures flanking the salvers, with their series of eccentric circles, were being used for this purpose. A 1688 inventory of the wealthy Yorkshire merchant Michael Warton records in the pantry:

1 Doz. of beer & wyne glasses
6 sack glasses (pro) salver
6 crewetts (pro) vineg(a)r
1 large crewett (pro) oyle
1 glass standard (pro) crewetts
2 water bottles

Among the Warton silver were '6 salvers' and '2 stands (pro) middle of the table', with a further two stands appearing in the list of pewter. The rest of the plate in Lamb's table plan, some 52 pieces in all, for serving the first and second courses, is all circular in shape and comes in five standard sizes. It is also possible that some platters may have been elevated using dish-stands or rings to 'make the fest look full and noble'.

Flanking the pyramid of sweetmeats, in place of the crewett stands, are two pairs of gilded candlesticks, which embody the prevalent styles of the second half of the seventeenth century. The simple cylindrical pair, with their collar drip-plates, are typical of *c.*1650, while the more elaborate examples, with chased raised octagonal bases and Gothic-style cluster columns, were made for the 1st Duke of Leeds by Jacob Bodendick in 1675.

FIG. 25
Design for a wild boar pie from Kidder's *Pastry and Cookery* – the dark hatching on the print was probably intended to indicate gilding

FIG. 26
A wild boar pie made to Kidder's design

FIG. 27
An illustration by Wenceslaus Hollar from *Æsop's Fables* (London 1668), edited by John Ogilby (1600–76)

A seventeenth-century pantry containing pies and roast meats. At this time pies were not served in slices as they are today; the lid was cut open and diners helped themselves to the contents with a spoon. Here a large pasty broken into in this way is intricately decorated with strapwork decorations similar to those on contemporary plaster ceilings. Two florendines (open-topped tarts) can be seen in the shadows on the back shelf. The large round pie at the rear of the pantry has a chimney for pouring in either clarified butter, if it was to be kept cold, or a lear or caudle if it was to be served hot. Behind the mice is a chine of beef, spiked with rosemary and cloves. The roasted fowl also appears to be spiked with cloves rather than larded. The cheese standing on its side on the shelf could very well be parmesan, which was popular at this time. It was an important ingredient of the 'Jacobin's pottage' a rich soup which first appeared in *The Queens Closet Open'd* (1655), a collection of recipes allegedly compiled by Queen Henrietta Marie.

FIG. 28
Chinese armorial dinner plate,
*c.*1715 (Xangxi period)
Diameter: 23 cm

When Samuel Tyssen, a wealthy London merchant living in what was then the rural village of Hackney, was granted arms in 1687, he used his trading connection to commission a splendid armorial dinner service. The Chinese manufacturer of this dinner plate has adopted the fashionable Japanese Imari style of decoration. Until this time Chinese porcelain was used chiefly for the banquet course of a meal. In the 1675 edition of her *Queen-like Closet* the Hackney-based cookery writer Hannah Wooley tells us that plates for sweetmeats 'must not be as broad as Trencher plates at Meat, and should be either of Silver or China'. The earliest Chinese armorial dinner service for the British market was made for Governor Pitt of Madras in about 1705.

FIG. 29
Dish, armorial supper set (centre section),
*c.*1724 (Yongzheng period)
Diameter: *c.*12 cm

Hannah Wooley described kaleidoscopic arrangements of small china dishes for serving sweetmeats as early as 1675. Reminiscent of the interlocking pie designs of the period, these were usually arranged on a wooden dessert frame. These luxury items were available only to those who could afford them. This central star of a composite supper set, which would have been completed with wedge-shaped dishes, has the quarterly arms of a second surviving son of Belasyse of York – probably the younger brother of Thomas, 4th Viscount Fauconberg, from Newburgh Priory. In 1723 John Nott was advising those readers of his *Cook's and Confectioner's Dictionary* who could not afford such prestigious arrangements:

> *For want of China Dishes, Tin-moulds in the same Shapes may be used; which will not be easily discovered, the Bottoms ought always to be covered with Leaves or Paper, before anything is dress'd upon them.*

FIG. 30
Blue-and-white delftware punch bowl, English, *c.*1730
Height: 18.2 cm
Diameter: 35 cm

This English delftware punch bowl, probably made in Bristol, clearly shows the response of native potters to the enormous quantity of imported Chinese porcelain at this time. The central circular reserve shows a farmer ploughing the fields beside a cottage, with a church in the distance. It is inscribed: IOSEPH SPRINGHALL : WHOLE : SALE : POTTER : IN : MATTSHALL [*sic*] : IN : THE : COUNTY : OF : NORFOLK. The charming rural scene in an obviously European style contrasts with the Chinese-influenced decorations on the outside of the bowl. Punch itself seems to have been another oriental importation. Its name is derived from Hindi *panch* (five), supposedly referring to its five ingredients: spirits, water, sugar, spice and lemon juice. Perhaps the original owner of the punch bowl would have used it for serving the Duke of Norfolk's Punch, a local variant on the theme. Although many punches were served hot – special punch kettles were used to heat the water – some were preferred chilled, or even frozen in the form of 'punch water ice'. A particularly luxurious ice of this kind called punch Romaine became popular in the 1820s. It was made from champagne, brandy and maraschino blended into a mousse with Italian meringue and then chilled in a pewter freezing pot.

CHAPTER 2

Dinner is Served

FIG. 31
A re-creation of a seventeenth-century banquet of sweetmeats

In his *English Housewife* (1615) Gervase Markham describes how an after-course of marchpanes, fruit pastes, marmalades, wafers and comfits should be embellished with 'a dish made for shew only, as Beast, Bird, Fish, fowl, according to invention'.[1] The dish 'for shew only' here is a marchpane based on knot garden designs from William Lawson's *Country Housewife's Garden* (1627) surrounding a 'sugar plate' replica of the banqueting house at Long Melford Hall (*c*.1570). Other 'banqueting matters' are arranged on novelty sugar plates, dishes and tazze. Sixteenth-century Italian recipe books introduced the English to the novel idea of edible sugar 'platters, glasses, cups and such like things, wherewith you may furnish a table, and when you have done, eat them up. A pleasant thing for them that sit at the table.'[2] The other sweetmeats in the display, from early seventeenth-century recipes, include boxes of cotoniake, printed white and red quince marmalade struck with long comfits, moulded gingerbreads, and jumbalds in the form of knots and letters. In *Delights for Ladies* (1600) Sir Hugh Platt tells us how 'our comfit makers at this day make their letters, knots, Armes, escocheons, beasts, birds, and other fancies'.[3] In 1617 John Murrell gives a recipe to make the letters, although in our display the designs are taken from the paintings of Clara Peeters.[4] The damask tablecloth (*c*.1600) is decorated with scenes from the legend of Bel and the Dragon.

AT TIMES when there has been sufficient to fill the pot, the poor have always been content to enjoy their food with the minimum of fuss. Apart from simple but dignified displays of pious gratitude, epitomized by the family saying grace in Joseph van Aken's painting of *c*.1725 (fig. 2), elaborate codes of etiquette have rarely loomed large in working-class food culture. To the rich and powerful, however, dining has customarily been much more than simply sharing good food in pleasant company. 'In an aristocratical country like England, not the Trial by Jury, but the dinner, is the capital institution,' wrote R. W. Emerson in the 1850s, marvelling at the way an Englishman's rank in society could immediately be revealed by the way he held his fork.[5] To class-conscious Victorians the manner in which one partook of dinner was considered an important gauge of civilized behaviour:

> *It is not a dinner at which sits the aboriginal Australian, who gnaws his bone half bare and then flings it behind to his squaw. Dining is the privilege of civilization. The rank which a people occupy in the grand scale may be measured by their way of taking their meals. The nation which knows how to dine has learnt the leading lesson of progress.*[6]

Isabella Beeton, at her most pompous when she wrote these words of haughty imperial snobbery, would no doubt be shocked to see the informal style of dining that so many of her countrymen had adopted by the end of the twentieth century. That modern equivalent of her 'aborigine's half gnawed bone', the takeaway in front of the telly, has become the norm for many. And what would she have made of the solitary diner with her hot dog in Colin Self's depiction of a 1960s fast-food bar (fig. 32)?

Despite much more relaxed attitudes to dining today, most of us still relish the sense of occasion created by elegant cutlery, glass and table linen. An

FIG. 32
Colin Self (b.1941), *Fall-Out Shelter Series (Infra-Red Frankfurt Roast and Eater)*, 1965
Pencil, coloured pencil and collage on paper
53.5 × 39 cm

This is one of a series of drawings known as the Fall-out Shelter Series that Self produced in 1965 following a visit to the United States. The characteristic feature of all the works is the fall-out shelter sign, an emblematic reminder of the threat of nuclear war as experienced during the Cold War. In this particular work, a woman eating a hot dog is represented in front of a sausage grill. By emphasizing the phallic connotations of the hot dog, the drawing conflates the consumption of food with sex. The inclusion of the shelter sign, with its implicit threat of nuclear destruction, gives a sinister edge to this representation of a young woman indulging in fast food – itself a potent reminder of the influence of American popular culture on British eating habits from the 1960s onwards.

appetizing display of food, above all, remains as important to us now as it was to Gervase Markham in the early seventeenth century, when he instructed the housewives of England in the skills of laying out a great feast. In *The English Housewife* (1615) he explains how food for important occasions was served and arranged in noble households. His aim in writing the book was to help gentlewomen lower down the social order to imitate the fashionable tables of their superiors. The recommended style of presentation is markedly different from the way our food is served today. At that time diners usually sat down to a meal of two courses, both of them rather like buffets of many different dishes arranged symmetrically before them on the table (see figs 15, 16 & 33). They chose which dishes they wanted to sample from the large selection on offer. Markham explains how the various dishes were brought to table, telling the housewife that 'she should first marshall her Sallets, delivering the Grand Sallet first'.[7] This opening dish was usually a highly embellished salad of many different ingredients, which could include olives, capers, samphire, barberries and currants as well as green salad herbs and flowers. One recipe suggests cowslip buds, violet flowers, strawberry leaves and brooklime. A sprig of rosemary or some other decorative 'standard' was frequently used as an embellishment. These decorations were as seasonal as the ingredients: 'Remember that in Autumn, your Standard ought to be the Resemblence of a Castle, carv'd out of Carrots and Turnips: in the Winter a Tree hung with Snow: in Summer a green Tree.'[8] Some 'grand sallets' with great central plumes of embellished rosemary are just visible behind the serving hatch of the kitchen in Hoefnagel's *Wedding Fête at Bermondsey* (see fig. 4 and detail, fig. 5).

Markham continues listing the order in which the other dishes of the first course were to be put before the guests:

> *And being thus Marshalled from the Dresser, the Sewer upon the placing them on the Table, shall not set them down as he received them, but Setting the sallets extravagently about the table, mixe the Fricases about them: then the boyled meats amongst the Fricases, rost meats amongst the boyled, bak't meats amongst the rost, and Carbanadoes amongst the bak'd, so that before every trencher may stand a sallet, a Fricase, a boyled meat, a rost meat, a bak'd meat, and a carbonado, which will give a most comely beauty to the Table, and very great contentment to the Guests.*[9]

This huge selection of food was followed by an equal number of second-course dishes, consisting mainly of roasted birds and fish dishes that could be prepared quickly while the guests ate the first course. Drinks were served from the side-board (see fig. 33 opposite).

This manner of presenting food, which later became known as service *à la Française*, had been customary in England since medieval times and remained standard practice until the nineteenth century. Guests were not expected to eat everything, but simply to choose their preferred dishes from the large display on the table before them. This is perfectly illustrated in an account of a dinner attended in 1822 by George IV in Edinburgh, where out of twenty first-course dishes he chose only four (see pp.87–8). At this time some were beginning to consider this 'common custom of setting out a table, with a parade and a profusion', though exciting to the appetite, extremely wasteful. Dr William Kitchener, in *The Cook's Oracle* of 1823, advocated a simpler style of dining:

> *Such pompous preparation, instead of being a compliment to our Guests, is nothing better than an indirect offence; it is a tacit insinuation, that it is absolutely necessary to provide such delicacies to bribe the depravity of their palates, when we desire the pleasure of their company.*[10]

The doctor would have approved of the new style of dining, *service à la Russe*, that was becoming fashionable in France during his lifetime. This eventually spread to England, where by the reign of Victoria it had become the standard method of regulating a table (which remains in use today). A smaller number of dishes were served in a fixed order, one after the other, leaving plenty of room in the middle of the table for decorations.

Kitchener was particularly scornful of the British love of sweet puddings and that sugary adjunct to the dinner, the dessert:

> *It is your senseless second courses – ridiculous variety of wines, desserts, ices, liqueurs &c. – which are served up merely to feed the Eye, or pamper palled appetite, that overcome the Stomach, and paralyse Digestion, and seduce 'children of a larger Growth' to sacrifice the health and comfort of several days, – for the Baby-pleasure of tickling their tongue for a few minutes, with Trifles and Custards!*[11]

FIG. 33
Detail from an illustration in Francis Sandford's *History of the Coronation of James II* (London 1687)

Prepared by the king's master cook Patrick Lamb, this feast perfectly illustrates service à la Française, with drinks being served from the court cupboards. In the top left hand corner of the nearest table there is a 'spiked' or larded chine similar to that depicted in Hollar's etching of a pantry (fig. 27). On the far right of the fourth row of plates on the same table there is a charger which appears to be a filled with the fashionable shaped pies of the period. Although the artist has gone to some trouble to illustrate these foods, his dishes do not match those shown on Sandford's table plan, a detail of which is reproduced in fig. 15. Despite the magnificence of Lamb's extravagant creation, soon after the feast the newly crowned king replaced him with a French cook (see p.38).

FIG. 34
Gerrit Houckgeest (*c.*1600–1661),
Charles I, Queen Henrietta Maria and Charles, Prince of Wales, Dining in Public, 1635
Oil on panel, 63.2 × 92.4 cm

Reminiscent of Veronese's monumental set pieces, this painting of the Stuart royal family dining in front of selected guests offers some valuable insights into the complexities of service associated with seventeenth-century aristocratic meals. The conventions of serving at the royal table had been well established by the late medieval period, when the monarch was waited on by high-ranking courtiers favoured with important household positions. It was then considered a great honour to carve the king's meat, serve his wine, or even gather up the leftovers in a voiding basket at the end of the meal. Each function was carried out by a gentleman officer of the household who had a special role, the most important being that of the Sewer, whose task it was to superintend the arrangement of the table, the seating of the guests and the serving of the food. By the reign of Charles these titles had become symbolic, so that on a daily basis food tended to be served by professional attendants, although the gentlemen officers of the household came into their own at important ceremonial meals, such as marriage feasts and coronations.

Here a sewer and a carver can be seen attending the royal family, while the butler carefully carries a cup to be replenished with the wine that is cooling in a great cistern by the side table. A retinue of ushers entering from the servery bring yet more dishes to a board that already appears overloaded.

FIG. 35
A reconstruction at Howsham Hall, York, of the garden arbour structure shown in the early seventeenth-century wall painting illustrated opposite

FIG. 36
Anon, *Return of the Prodigal Son*, c.1600
Wall painting, 75 × 110 cm

Painted some time between 1600 and 1620, this naïve yet vigorous wall painting shows the prodigal son carousing with harlots in an arbour in the garden of a tavern or brothel. Two liveried waites playing shawms are entertaining the party with loud outdoor music while the landlady reckons up the bill on her slate.

In a passage in his *Anatomy of Abuses* (1583) – which could almost serve as a caption to this painting – the puritan preacher Philip Stubbes disapprovingly describes a similar scene of debauchery:

> *In the Feeldes and Suburbes of the Cities thei have Gardens, either pailed, or walled around about very high, with their Harbers and Bowers fit for the purpose. And least thei might be espied in these open places, thei have their Banquetting Houses with Galleries, turrettes, and what not els therin sumptuously erected; wherin thei maie (and doubtlesse doe) Many of them plaie the filthie persons ... truly I think some of these places are little better than the Stewes and Brothell Houses were in tymes past.*[12]

In a scene being enacted behind, the prodigal is being chased by two maids, one with a broom, the other with a spit, while a third empties the slops over his head.

The composition of this raucous scene is very similar to a number of early seventeenth-century continental treatments of the same subject, the best known of which is attributed to the Antwerp painter Frans Pourbus the Elder (1545–81). However, this English fresco seems to be derived loosely from a widely distributed print of 1608 relating to the parable of the prodigal son, etched by Claes Janz Vischer (1587– 1652) and based on a design by David Vincboons (1576–1632), which features a garden bower covered in luxuriant vines.[13]

'Bowers of bliss' of this kind were probably quite common garden features, but few could compete with the temporary banqueting house Queen Elizabeth had erected in Greenwich Park in 1560:

> *... made with fir poles and decked with birch branches and all manner of flowers both of the field and of the garden; as roses, july flowers, lavender, marygolds and all manner of strewing herbs and rushes.*[14]

The dessert has an extraordinary history. Its origins lie in a medieval ceremony known as the *voidée* or void, which took place at the end of important court meals.[15] After grace the sovereign was offered sweet spiced wine (hippocras) and wafers as part of a thanksgiving, a ritual with obvious echoes of the holy eucharist. However, the main purpose of the *voidée* was medicinal, as the warming spices of the hippocras were believed to help settle the stomach and prevent indigestion. For this reason sugar-coated seeds and spices (comfits) with digestive and carminative properties were also served. By the sixteenth century this practice had become widespread among the nobility and high-ranking clergy. At the Italian papal and humanist courts this ultimate course was served from the *credenza* or sideboard. Boxes of quince paste (*cotognata in scatoline*) and other preserves, as well as a remarkably wide range of sugared seeds, candied roots and flowers – even perfumed toothpicks – were offered to the guests.[16]

A growing enthusiasm among the Tudors for the new culture pioneered by the Italian humanist courts led to adoption of these modish foods in Britain, so that the customary hippocras, wafers and spices came to be augmented by many new luxury sweets of Mediterranean origin. When they were in season, fresh fruit and cream cheeses were also served. The rapid spread of distillation during the sixteenth century meant that a wide range of strong alcoholic cordial waters joined or replaced the hippocras as after-dinner drinks; among them were surfeit waters for easing the stomach pains of the overindulgent. This expanded version of the void became known in England as the banquet (from the Italian word *banchetto*). Continental names for the confectionery items, which were imported from Spain and Portugal as well as from Italy, were also retained, although they were soon anglicized – quince paste became known as cotonigac or marmalet (from Portuguese *marmelo* – quince), while the all-important comfits derived their name from the Italian *confetti*. In a book of banquet recipes published in 1617, the cook and confectioner John Murrell included many recipes for confectionery of obvious southern European origin, including callishones, muschachones, muscadinoes, canalones, gentilissoes and novellissoes.[17]

Like the hippocras and the comfits, quince paste was considered to have a calming effect on a tormented digestion, 'some make a confection of Quinces, called Marmalade, which is verie soveraigne against a flux of the bellie'.[18] John Parkinson, herbarist to James I, wrote with great enthusiasm of the culinary delights and medicinal properties of this luxurious fruit:

FIG. 37
Master of the Countess of Warwick (active second half of sixteenth century), *William Brooke, 10th Lord Cobham and his Family*, 1570?
(Devonshire Collection version)
Oil on canvas, 125 × 153 cm

There are two surviving versions of this painting (this one from the Devonshire Collection, the other at Longleat) showing William Brook and his family enjoying a fruit banquet in the company of the family pets. Both show a table laid with a variety of fruit and nuts. Although physicians believed the consumption of fresh fruit caused 'fluxes', here is ample proof that it was eaten by some with relish.

FIG. 38
Detail from the Longleat version of the Cobham family group

An interesting gastronomical detail appears only in the Longleat version of this family group – the plate of long comfits illustrated below. A popular sweet of the period, these were made by coating narrow strips of cinnamon or candied orange peel with sugar in a balancing pan. Their somewhat crinkled appearance earned them the name 'ragged' or 'pearled' comfits. In the Devonshire Collection version (right) a portrait of Lord Cobham's youngest son George has been added to the foreground, obscuring that part of the table with the plate of comfits.

FIG. 39
Anon, *Banquet in Egyptian Hall of London Guildhall with parterre dessert* (before 1796)
Etching, 30 × 20 cm

Although there are written accounts of French-style garden desserts (such as the description by Parson Woodforde of one he saw during a dinner at the Bishop of Norwich's house in 1783), this is the only known English image of such a setting, which may represent the dessert course of a dinner given in 1773 for John Wilkes. Continental confectioners based in London were responsible for introducing this elegant style of parterre dessert, which by the 1760s was replacing earlier pyramidal arrangements (see fig. 17). The sculpture on the table plateau could have been made from either sugar paste, wax or porcelain and it was possible to hire all three kinds from city confectionery shops. Although the table is laid with a profusion of syllabub or jelly glasses, ice cream was becoming increasingly popular in London at this time. In his Court and Country Confectioner (1770), Borella (private confectioner to the Spanish ambassador) gives recipes for cream ices of brown bread and elderflower, as well as directions to make ices in the shapes of fruits.

FIG. 40
Detail of a late baroque dessert (*c.*1749) re-created at Fairfax House, York, for the exhibition *Pleasures of the Table* (1997)

Decorative parterres were a popular feature of plateau dessert settings from around 1749 onwards. The fashion originated in France but rapidly became an international craze, having spread as far as the Ottoman court by the late 1760s. The parterre cases were made either from mousseline, a moss-like sugar paste pressed through a sieve, or from pasteboard covered in chenille, velvet or baize. They were filled with coloured sugars. Later in the century the sugars, or sometimes coloured marble dust, were sprinkled directly onto mirror plateaux in swirling cants and volutes.

> *There is no fruit growing in this Land that is of so many excellent uses as this, serving as well to make many dishes of meate for the table, as for banquets, and much more for the Physicall vertues ... And being preserved whole in Sugar, either white or red, serve likewise, not onely as an after dish to close up the stomacke, but is placed among other Preserves by Ladies and Gentlewomen, and bestowed on their friends to entertaine them, and among other sorts of Preserves at Banquets. Codimacke also and Marmilade, Ielly and Paste, are all made of Quinces, chiefly for delight and pleasure, although they also have with them some physicall properties.*[19]

How these expensive confections were made was a mystery to most and there was a great deal of curiosity as to how they could be imitated at home. The publication in London in 1558 of a translation of an Italian recipe book by Girolamo Ruscelli (*The Secrets of Maister Alexis of Piedmont*) revealed for the first time how professionals made a whole range of confectionery and distilled waters, enabling English gentlewomen to concoct their own with produce from their orchards and gardens.

From the Restoration onwards French methods of presentation became fashionable and dessert settings often featured tall pyramids of fruit and sweetmeats, a style made popular by the court of Louis XIV (see figs 3 & 22). By the early eighteenth century the French name *dessert* was replacing that of banquet, and from mid-century onwards smart English tables were decorated in the continental manner, with centrepieces of parterre gardens with sugar or porcelain figures (see frontispiece and figs 39 & 40).

Table plans for plateau garden desserts were still being published in the 1820s, when Kitchener was advising the public that 'the Vigour of Manhood seeketh not to be sucking Sugar, or sipping Turtle'.[20] Perhaps at no other time in the history of English food has the contrast between the diet of the rich and the poor been so great as it was at this time. While the smart set dined in luxury on turtle soup and *ponche à la Régence*, the poor queued for handouts of coarse bread at parish doles. In the following two essays the simple bread-based diet of the poor is contrasted with a highly refined aristocratic style of dining developed during the Regency.

FIG. 41
Anon, *Lazarus and Dives*, sixteenth-century rectangular sycamore trencher
Oil on panel, 12 × 15 cm

Although other rectangular examples have survived, fruit trenchers were more usually made in the form of thin wooden roundels about five inches in diameter. They are frequently decorated on the back with knotwork patterns and images and inscribed with verses, mottoes or scriptural texts. It is likely that guests ate their sweetmeats and comfits from the plain unpainted side during the banquet course. Apparently they were sometimes made of sugar paste. In *The Art of English Poesie* (1589) William Puttenham informs us:

> *There be also another like epigrams that were sent usually for new yeare's gifts, or to be printed or put upon banketting dishes of sugar plate, or of March paines, &c., they were called Nenia or Apopherata, and never contained above one verse, or two at the most, but the shorter the better. We call them poesies, and do paint them upon the back sides of our fruit-trenchers of wood.*[21]

What appears to be a 'sugar plate' trencher is depicted in *Lazarus and the Rich Man's Table* (1618) by Gasper van der Hoekenn.[22]

The trencher illustrated here is one of three of a very high quality, which appear to be the only survivors from a larger set. Unlike the more common roundels with their knotted embellishments, all are painted with biblical scenes enclosed in mannerist strapwork borders with verses in an Italianate hand. The designs were probably traced from woodcuts by the German artist Virgil Solis, whose illustrations to the Old and New Testaments were published in *Biblische Figuren* in Frankfurt in 1565.[23]

Dives dines in splendour with his smart friends in a banqueting house covered with gold embroidered textiles, while the semi-naked Lazarus begs at the palace gate. However, the accompanying verse warns of an imminent reversal of roles, which the miniaturist has depicted to the right of the banqueting house:

> *The Lazar pore on yearth had paine:*
> *But after deathe hath Joy and reste:*
> *The glotten riche had pleasures vaine*
> *And after deathe hathe hell posseste*

The other two trenchers from the set illustrate *Jonah and the Whale* and *The Harvest of the World*, food and drink themes also designed to remind the banqueteer of the vanity of riches and transient pleasures. Vanitas themes and admonitions against gluttony and drunkenness frequently occur in verses on more conventional roundels, for example:

> *Though hungrie meales be put in pot*
> *Yet conscience cleare keept without*
> *spot*
> *Doth keepe ye corpse in quiet rest*
> *Than hee that thousandes hathe in*
> *chest*

Spelt out clearly on the very trencher from which the luxury sweetmeats were eaten at the end of the meal, these reminders of the consequences of gluttony must have left the overindulgent with a strong sense of unease about the fate of their immortal souls.

LVKE XVI
This Lazar pore on yearth had payne:
but after deathe hath Ioy and reste:
The glotton riche had pleasures vayne
and after deathe hath hell posseste:

FIG. 42
Marcellus Laroon (1679–1772)
Dessert being served at a Dinner Party, 1725
Oil on canvas, 91.4 × 86 cm

This conversation piece by Captain Marcellus Laroon, a soldier and musician who painted for his own pleasure, shows a group of lively young aristocrats consuming a fruit dessert. The nobleman wearing the blue riband of the garter who appears to be the host has been variously identified as Frederick, the Prince of Wales, The Duke of Wharton or the Duke of Montagu.[24] Whatever his true identity, he is gaining a great deal of satisfaction from pouring a long stream of dessert wine from a fiasco. A well-dressed child, who does not appear to be a servant, is assisting by distributing the drinks from a footed salver. A footman concentrates carefully as he steers through the guests with a pyramid of fruit embellished with a coronet of flowers. Pyramids made of dried fruits and sweetmeats were decorated at this time in the French mode, with *fleurs contrefaites ou artificielles* skilfully made from silk, paper or coloured sugar paste. In a contemporary English confectionery text plagiarized from the standard French work on desserts, *Nouvelle instruction pour les confitures, les liqueurs et les fruits* (1692), we are told that:

> *the Tops of the Pyramids of dryed Fruits, may be garnished with these Artificial Flowers; or else a separate Nosegay may be made of them, for the Middle of your Desert; or they may be laid in Order in a Basket, or kind of Cup, made of fine Pastry-work of Crackling-Crust, neatly cut and dry'd for that purpose.*[25]

FIG. 43
Wafers and gingerbread figures

The wafers shown above, made from flour, sugar and cream spiced with cinnamon, were made in a pair of early seventeenth-century wafering irons (courtesy of the Bowes Museum). Wafers of this kind were usually served with hippocras and comfits during the banquet course, or at wedding and christening celebrations. The figures shown on the left are made from 'white gingerbread', a spicy breadcrumb mix encased in a sugar-paste coating. The finely carved boxwood moulds from which they have been 'printed' (courtesy of the Pinto Collection) date from the mid-seventeenth century.

Fig. 44
Minton cream tureen, bone china, 1851
Height: 32 cm

Part of the Minton dessert service bought by Queen Victoria at the Great Exhibition of 1851, this 'cream tureen' was one of four decorated with Parian figures and exotic flower, fruit and bird designs that caught her attention. It was intended for serving preserves in syrup and brandy fruits.

Fig. 45
Minton dessert plate, bone china, *c.*1867
Diameter: 23 cm

It is hard to imagine anyone gluttonous enough to obscure with a helping of fruit the delicately hand-painted decoration in the centre of this plate, part of a dessert service produced to commemorate the safe return of Lord Milton and his companions from an eighteen-month expedition to the North-West Passage in 1862–3. Seated on the left amidst the rugged rocks and fir trees, just identifiable by his red headband, our noble lord contemplates an attempt to cross the rapids in a near-capsized canoe, while his faithful friend and photographer Walter Butler Cheadle observes the drama through a telescope, prior to taking one of the many photographs from which the Minton artists worked to recreate the adventures which appealed so much to the popular imagination.

FIG. 46
Napkin, linen damask, Scottish?, *c.*1830
Dimensions: 92 × 79 cm
Design woven with exotic birds

Ornithology was very popular around 1800 and a number of extensive studies were published, notably in Paris and London. It is significant that the famous bird artist Audubon chose London to publish the first volume of *Birds of America* in 1827. The field of this napkin has a pair of crowned cranes, with lyrebirds in the four corners. Both species are depicted performing an elaborate courtship display. There are a number of other linen damask designs from this period showing both exotic and European birds.

FAR RIGHT:
FIG. 49
Napkin, linen damask, Scottish, *c.*1850
Dimensions: 80 × 79 cm
Probably woven for the Crystal Palace Exhibition of 1851

The *Art-Journal Illustrated Catalogue* of the Great Exhibition included a tablecloth with the identical portrait of the Queen and its surround. Manufactured by a Mr Birrell of Dunfermline from a design by Joseph Neil Paton, it was described as 'bold and elaborate in design, and in all respects worthy of covering a regal table'.

Fig. 47
A modern linen napkin, folded according to instructions in Mattia Giegher's *Trattato sul modo di piegare, li tre trattati* (Padova 1639)

Fig. 48
Detail from an illustration of napkin-folding designs in Giegher's book cited above. The techniques for folding napkins into fantastic shapes set out by Giles Rose in *A Perfect School of Instructions for the Officers of the Mouth* in 1682 were almost certainly based on those illustrated by Giegher more than forty years earlier. Giegher's designs ranged in complexity from simple crimped pyramids to a standing lion and a double-headed eagle. The bird shown here was one of his most successful designs and is still used today at banquets in the royal palaces of Austria.

By Bread Alone?

Fig. 50
James Lobley (1828–88),
The Dole at Stowe Church, 1869
Oil on canvas, 50 x 71 cm

This touching scene of high-minded Anglican charity appeals on many levels. As a demonstration of generosity to the deserving poor, its theme would have been a comforting one for Lobley's wealthy patrons. On the other hand, nineteenth-century antiquarian preoccupations with folklore and paganism invite us to compare this homely church distribution of bread to ancient offerings to the grain goddess. On a much simpler level it gives us a clear idea of the appearance of the nineteenth-century quartern or four-pound loaf (see p. 119).

'DOST THOU think, because thou art virtuous, there shall be no more cakes and ale?' asks Sir Toby Belch of Feste, the clown in *Twelfth Night*. Sir Toby did not have Black Forest gateau or Victoria sponge in mind but was probably thinking of something like a teacake or a hot cross bun. Shakespeare implied that cakes were not for those of moral integrity – cakes were frivolous, whereas bread was a staple necessity. But these two foods represented extremes of a continuum, linked by the common method of kneading flour into dough and leavening it by allowing it to ferment. 'Fermentation' describes the action of yeast cells in baking, converting sugar into alcohol and carbon dioxide, which is also essential to the brewing of ale and beer. The crafts of baker and brewer were closely linked, the latter providing yeast for some types of bread.

Poor or wealthy, rural or urban, everyone ate some form of bread as a staple. The better-off ate it as one element in a diet that included copious amounts of meat, fish and other nutritious foods, while poor people frequently had little of anything. Joseph van Aken's *Grace before a Meal* (fig. 2) was painted at a time of relative plenty for all, but it does not convey the impression that an ample meal is about to be consumed by the humble group depicted. It was not unusual for bread alone to be the experience of the poor, both rural and urban. Starvation was often just around the corner, and never more consistently than in the early nineteenth century. The presence of scarcity and privation at that time was rife, and it existed against a backdrop of social change in which the white wheaten loaf was emerging as the most sought-after form of bread.

Present-day emphasis on wheat bread as a staple in the English diet is misleading in the longer-term historical context. Before the wheaten loaf became commonplace, numerous cereals were used according to differences in topography and climate, social class and custom. In 1587 Holinshed remarked:

> *The bread throughout the land is made of such graine as the soil yeeldeth ... the gentilitie commonlie prouide themselves sufficientlie*

> *of wheate for their owne tables, whilest their household and poore neighbours in some shires are inforced to content themselves with rie, or barlie, yea, and in time of derth, manie with bread made either of beans, peason or otes, or of altogether and some acornes among, which scourge the poorest doo soonest tast.*[26]

As well as bread, these grains made other foods and beverages – pottages (stews of grain or oatmeal in milk or broth), frumenty, puddings, beers.

At this time wheat breads were defined both by the quality of the flour and by the chosen leavening agent. In 1615 Gervase Markham listed three basic types.[27] Manchet required finest white flour, kneaded with barm – froth taken from the top of fermenting ale or beer, full of active yeast cells. It was shaped into small round loaves, which after baking weighed about six ounces each, and was the best bread. The ordinary quality of bread was known as chet or cheat bread. This was made from flour that retained some bran, mixed with sour leaven (dough kept from the previous baking) boosted with barm. Both manchet and chet were eaten by the better-off; they were specified for meals of the upper ranks of the nobility and higher officials at the Court in 1526.[28] The coarsest was maslin or monkecorne bread, made for the hinds (farm labourers). The word 'maslin' denotes a mixture of grain, often wheat and rye or wheat and barley. Markham's recipe included barley, pease, wheat or rye, and malt, ground to meal and mixed with hot water in a 'sower trough' – a wooden kneading trough cleaned only by scraping, so that yeast cells remained in the residue clinging to the wood, ready to multiply when the trough was next used. Maslin was made up into 'greate loaues' and baked in strong heat.

Basic distinctions between wheat breads are only half the story, however. There was also considerable regional diversity in types of bread grain. Discussing the use of oatmeal, Markham commented that 'in diverse Countries [counties] six seuerall kinds of very good and wholesome bread, eury one finer than the other, as your Anacks, Ianacks, and such like' were made.[29] He also referred to various oatcakes, some of which he considered extremely fine. Oats were particularly important in the north and west of the British Isles; the Welsh and the people of the north-west Midlands, West Yorkshire, Lancashire, the Lake District and Scotland devised myriad forms of oat bread or cake. The West Yorkshire variety was 'havercake', a thin floppy oatcake made with sour leaven. In the Lake District, in the 1690s, Celia Fiennes reported that a thin, unleavened oat bread was made by 'clapping out' the dough (spreading it thinly with the heel of the hand) and drying it on a girdle. In parts of Scotland, loaves of wheat bread were apparently unusual in the eighteenth century. Squire Matthew Bramble described a Scottish breakfast that included 'a bushel of oatmeal made into thin cakes and bannocks; with a small wheaten loaf in the middle, for the strangers'.[30] Many oat breads survived well into the nineteenth century, when 'jannock', an unleavened oat bread containing dried fruit, presumably a descendant of Markham's 'Ianack', was still known in the Bolton area. To this day three forms of oatcake are still made: biscuity Scottish types, thrown oatcakes of the Pennine valleys and soft oatcakes of the Staffordshire Potteries.

Large, heavy rye loaves mixed in a dough trough were still remembered in the North Riding of Yorkshire as late as 1800. Maslin loaves were still made in the north-east of England at this time and may have been the model for the sturdy-looking loaf of brown household bread depicted by Mary Ellen Best (working in York in 1838) in *Still Life with Peeled Orange*. Cassell's *Universal Cookery Book* of 1900 included a recipe for 'Yorkshire brown bread' of white flour mixed with rye and bran – perhaps the last faint echo of a baking tradition dating back to the middle ages. Barley bread was also made in many parts of western and northern Britain, especially the West Country, Wales and Scotland.

But these old fashioned, heavy breads were in retreat. By 1796, the people of Nottinghamshire said they were losing their 'rye teeth'.[31] Keats was lyrical about barley bread (spread with clotted cream) in his *Poems written at Teignmouth*, but agriculturalists reported that it was disappearing from Devon and Cornwall. Formerly a Cornish staple, it had apparently become confined to small farms by the end of the eighteenth century. Only in Scotland have barley bannocks (originally baked on a girdle) survived.

Viewed against a background of such heavy, tooth-challenging breads, small wheaten cakes suddenly stand out as luxuries. Simple manchet would have been a treat for poor people, but it also gave rise to the whole English tribe of small yeast-leavened buns, rolls and 'cakes', enriched with varying proportions of fat, egg, dried fruit and spices. Good Friday 'cross buns' (the 'hot' element of the name came later) were one example; a folk-belief held that bread baked on this holiest of days had special qualities. Texts from the early modern period also make frequent references to 'wigs' or 'wigges', apparently, in early forms, made from white bread dough enriched with a little butter.[32] These were often flavoured with caraway seeds.

Ale barm was a vital element in the making of these types of bread. In the Bolton area of Lancashire a basic form of small wheat bread is still called a

FIG. 51
Thomas Webster (1800–86),
Roast Pig, 1862
Oil on canvas, 73 × 118.5 cm

Respectable, happy and content with their lot, this rural family is behaving just as Thomas Webster and the clients who bought and enjoyed his paintings would wish. The quaint rustic interior, midsummer foliage and sunshine glimpsed through the sparklingly clean window, together with the general air of merry anticipation of the weekly treat of roast pork, make for a profoundly reassuring image of country life. The pig would have been cooked in the village bakery, in the dying heat of the oven after the bread had been drawn. This bread, on its own, would have been their staple fare for the rest of the week, eked out perhaps with some fatty bacon or dripping. The rosy-cheeked boy balancing on tiptoe on his stool to catch a glimpse of the pig, whose aromas have wafted ahead, seems brimful of health and vitality. But the hyperactive behaviour of these children might conceivably be paroxysms of hunger, rather than the animal spirits their betters profess to admire at a distance but inwardly wish to depress. This worthy couple would have experienced as small children the agricultural riots of the 1830s and the brutal repression that followed. The old woman might well be the widow of one of the wretched village labourers hanged or transported for smashing the farm machinery that deprived them of work. The proud father in this painting, as an agricultural labourer in full- or part-time employment, may have earned a wage as low as seven shillings a week. Roast pork in this context seems to be more a figment of a complacent, but perhaps slightly troubled, middle-class conscience than a true depiction of the condition of the agricultural labourer in the 1860s.

'barm cake'; the name would originally have distinguished it from bread or oatcake made with sour leaven. Barm was not easy to manage. Books on household management contain instructions on how to minimize bitterness in it and keep it viable. The problem of bitterness was exacerbated by the increasing use of hops in brewing during the sixteenth century. But good barm worked swiftly and lacked the sour flavour of leaven. Dough raised with it could be sweetened with sugar and flavoured with spice, the resulting cakes or buns serving as a considerable treat for high days and holy days. Hot cross buns are widely known, but many regional festive breads are also recorded – for example, singin' hinnies in the north-east, dough cakes and lardy cakes in the midlands and south, and the mothering buns eaten on mid-Lent Sunday in Bristol. The idea of these confections as special food for good times is embodied in the saffron-tinted revel buns of the West Country. A 'revel' (in Lancashire called a 'wake') was an anniversary feast to celebrate the dedication of a church, but revels or wakes were not necessarily sober occasions.

Sweetened, spiced doughs were also the origin of rich fruit cakes. Until the mid-nineteenth century, 'great cakes' – the forerunners of our Christmas cakes and wedding cakes – were mostly raised by adding ale barm. Even after chemical leavenings were introduced (bicarbonate of soda began to appear in recipes in the 1840s), many people, especially in rural areas, continued to use yeast.

For agricultural labourers, church festivals provided an opportunity for relaxation. An event that involved hard work but also good and plentiful food was harvest. This was the one time of the year when labourers could exercise some form of collective bargaining and negotiate better terms, including special food. This often included plenty of beef or mutton, beer and wheat bread. In addition to the standard loaf, sweeter cakes such as wigs were included in the bargain. In 1750 William Ellis described how 'To make Wigs for the Harvest-men the Hertfordshire Way' using flour, ale yeast, caraway seed and sugar made into a bread dough. They were kneaded up and baked at the mouth of a brick oven 'and this we generally do about six o'clock in the Evening, that they may be hot against the Men come home to supper from reaping, when we toss one each of these large Wigs to each Man for his dipping in a Bowl of Ale'.[33] Harvest was a time of hard work and worry, when the prospects for the next twelve months began to become apparent: good or bad yields, high or low quality, plenty or want. The sense of a job well done was reflected in relief and general merrymaking – hence, perhaps, another association between cakes, ale and lack of virtue.

The ordinary loaf was an essential part of the daily routine and it was bread, with its quasi-religious imagery as the staff of life, on which attention focused when food was scarce. By the sixteenth century, given a choice, the inhabitants of south-east England preferred white wheat bread. They refused anything else by the time of the Napoleonic wars, when there were several years of scarcity as a result of poor harvests and restricted imports. Even the better-off felt the consequences. In April 1796 James Woodforde, parson of Weston Longeville, near Norwich, dined at the house of neighbouring gentry. He subsequently recorded in his diary: 'No kind of Pastrey, no Wheat Flour made use of… the Bread all brown Wheat-Meal with one part in four of Barley Flour. The Bread was well made and eat very well indeed, may we never eat worse.'[34] The gentry could afford meat and fish when bread was scarce and if they felt the need to make a patriotic gesture by limiting their use of white wheat flour, the poor must have been faring very badly indeed.

It had been usual in some grain-growing areas of England for labourers and servants to board in the farmsteads, sharing, to some extent, the fortunes of their employers. By the time of the Napoleonic Wars it was increasingly common for labourers to live out in their own cottages, fending for themselves. At this time their average wage of ten or twelve shillings a week bought only enough bread for survival, and sometimes not even that. Suggestions that other grains, such as oats, be substituted for scarce and expensive wheat were simply disregarded. Whatever the population of northern England may have considered acceptable, the poor of the south and east wanted wheat.

This was the beginning of fifty years' privation and extreme hardship for the poor, although Woodforde did not live to see the growing poverty and disaffection that was to afflict the country as a whole. The Corn Law of 1815 protected landowners' incomes, inducing artificially high prices for bread and exacerbating the hunger suffered by the poor. Riots became common in towns, and, increasingly, in the countryside. In places landless labourers had lost their common rights and thus their ability to produce some of their own food. Under the terms of the Poor Laws they were often moved on from parish to parish and in Norfolk this culminated in 1816 with labourers rioting in Ely, Littleport, Downham Market, Norwich and Brandon. Their demands were for 'Cheap Bread, a Cheap Loaf, and Provisions Cheaper'.[35] Beer played its part in the insurrection, much of it being centred on inns and alehouses. Only the presence of the militia quelled the unrest; eventually, five men received death sentences and a further nine were transported to Australia.

One reaction to the plight of the poor was charity. This had been essential to the old moral economy, to which Parson Woodforde subscribed. Despite making occasional observations in his diary about the indigence of some recipients, Woodforde comes across as a humane and generous man. In February 1795, during an especially cold winter, he was sufficiently concerned about the poor of his parish to organize a collection, which paid for emergency distribution of bread and fuel. On 15 February he recorded over fifty shillings' worth of brown bread being given to the poor of the parish. Forty shillings' worth had been given out on the previous Tuesday and a further fifty shillings' worth was arranged for the following Sunday.

Woodforde's dole of bread was a one-off reaction to an extreme situation. Other bread doles were annual events, and some survive around the country to the present day. Most, such as the Biddenden Dole in Kent, were endowed with property or capital to provide money or food, usually bread, on a specified date. The Biddenden Dole still takes place on Easter Monday; it consists of a large loaf, some cheese, a special commemorative biscuit and (nowadays) two pounds of tea. (Ale was originally part of the charity, but consumption of it diminished during the eighteenth century as tea became a fashionable drink for everyone – a trend that was to be further influenced by the temperance movement.) Another famous dole is the Tichborne Dole in Hampshire. Besides helping the needy, doles were an excellent method of ensuring that one's name would be remembered. Some were distributed from the graveside on the anniversary of a death, echoing the pre-Reformation idea that prayers of the living helped ease the souls of the dead into heaven.

By the mid-Victorian era the notions of sober religion and the deserving poor who knew their place had become well established. Overt forms of selection for doles had always been practised, such as specifying that widows were to be recipients. James Lobley used his painting of *The Dole at Stowe Church* (fig. 50) to make a moral point about the gulf between the lifestyles of the pious wealthy and the deserving poor. *Distributing Left-overs to the Poor after the Lord Mayor's Banquet at the Guildhall, 1882* (fig. 13) depicts those fortunate few who had tickets entitling them to collect the leftovers. In times of extreme scarcity, no doubt any gift of food was welcome, but the contribution to the overall nutrition of the poor by doles cannot have been substantial. Some doles apparently became a focus for rowdy scenes around the end of the eighteenth century, which was perhaps just another symptom of the privation felt by the poor at this time.

FIG. 52
Eyre Crowe (1824–1910),
The Dinner Hour, Wigan, 1874
Oil on canvas, 76.3 × 107 cm

When the craggily handsome mill-owner in Elizabeth Gaskell's novel *North and South* saw the 'miserable black frizzle of a dinner – a greasy cinder of meat' that one of his workers was having for his meagre lunch, he got together with the outspoken union leader to organize good plain food for the hands, cooked on factory premises. Thus over a nice hot-pot came about an unhoped-for improvement in industrial relations. No such luck for these Wigan factory girls, who are taking advantage of a rare good day to eat their 'dinner' out of doors in spite of the east wind and the smoke-polluted sky. Their robust good looks and bright cheerful appearance is at variance with contemporary photographs and descriptions of the Lancashire cotton trade. It is hard to imagine that their diet of tea, bread and potatoes would have produced the golden complexions and rounded limbs of the maidens here, though the painting would have been reassuring to Robert Taylor, art collector and owner of the Victoria Mills, on the left. The servant problem in Wigan was understandably acute – in spite of low wages and appalling working conditions, these young women preferred the tough life of the mill to the subservience of domestic work.

The urban poor were in no doubt that the Corn Laws were a bad thing, but for their rural counterparts of the early nineteenth century these laws were the subject of some ambivalence. It was probably recognized that, despite high corn prices, the legislation did help to protect certain jobs. *The Workers on the Edgecumbe Estates* (Nicholas Condy, *c.*1840, Mount Edgecumbe Estate/City of Plymouth Museums and Art Gallery) are depicted at a time when the repeal of the Corn Laws had become inevitable, and with it a commitment to the transformation of the United Kingdom into a manufacturing state in which agriculture would take second place. As the farm labourers' world slipped gradually away from them, the tail end of this trend was captured by Flora Thompson in her trilogy *Lark Rise to Candleford*, based on her childhood in a poor hamlet in Oxfordshire during the 1880s. At that time harvest home was still celebrated with hams and sirloins and plum puddings – 'such a tapping of eighteen gallon casks and baking of plum loaves…'[36] – but Flora's father, a tradesman, not a labourer, remarks:

> *The farmer paid his men starvation wages all the year and thought he made it up to them by giving that one good meal.*[37]

A labourer's wages still stood at about ten shillings a week in the 1880s. The family income was stretched by growing vegetables, rearing a bacon pig, and gleaning in the fields after harvest to collect grain. These ingredients made a daily meal of a little bacon cooked with vegetables, potatoes and a suet pudding. Bought wheaten bread was the main component of all other meals, spread with home-rendered lard.

Although Flora Thompson's world seems timeless, her book was a retrospective view first published on the eve of the Second World War. Even by the time of the death of Queen Victoria in 1901, most people had minimal contact with a subsistence economy. Many labourers went from the land to fight in the First World War, and few returned. Of those who did, some found their jobs taken by machines. The rhythms and customs of urban life separated people from the origins of their foodstuffs.

FIG. 53
George Jones (1786–1869), *The Coronation Banquet of George IV*, 1821 (detail)
Oil on canvas, 110 × 90 cm

This view of the King on a raised dais, surrounded by the five Royal dukes and Prince Leopold, does much to capture the majesty of the occasion. As an accurate representation, however, it leaves much to be desired. A detailed plan of the table that has survived in the Royal Archives reveals a curiously antiquated mode of service at the King's table. A raised plateau, for example, probably blue and gold Sèvres, flanked by four gilded salts, was actually used and remained at the head of the table throughout the meal. Ices and ice pails were also in place during each course. For dessert there were '8 Assiettes montées in gold and glass, 17 plates of fruit, 4 comports, the comportier is central, 2 ices (ice pail-gold)', but pride of place in front of the king was given to 'a pineapple weighing ten and a half pounds'.

Regency Ragoos & Royal Service

FIG. 54
Napkin, linen damask, *c.*1808
Dimensions: 115 × 86 cm
Woven by J.W. Coulson, Lisburn, for the Prince Regent

The Irish linen-weavers had been supplying the English court with napery since the 1720s. This example was described as being of 'the largest size and superfine quality'. The border (not described in the Coulson invoice) consists of a superb scrolling acanthus leaf and passion flower design, which proved popular during the early years of the nineteenth century.

TO BE BORN into the wrong age was a great enough disappointment for George, Prince of Wales, but when also excluded from meaningful state duties by his overbearing, frugal and increasingly deranged father, King George III, it was perhaps not surprising that the future Prince Regent turned to the arts and architecture for fulfilment. His first major project, Carlton House, exercised his mind and the nation's pocket for over thirty years. When Horace Walpole, that great arbiter of fashion, saw the house in 1795 he was full of praise:

> *It is the taste and propriety that strike. Every ornament is at a proper distance, and not too large, but all delicate and new, with more freedom and variety than Greek ornaments and though probably borrowed from the Hôtel de Condé and other new palaces, not one that is not rather classic than French.*[38]

As a supporter of the arts the Prince of Wales received considerable acclaim and he was certainly one of the great royal patrons, ranking amongst such names as Henry VIII, Charles I and his grandfather, Frederick, Prince of Wales, who died in 1751. George's misfortune, however, was to be born at a time when the English royal family was being subjected to increasing scrutiny. As J. H. Plumb commented:

> *The extensions of literacy, the widespread dissemination of newspapers and above all the multiplicity of cheap coloured prints, drawn by some of the ablest and cruellest satirists that have ever lived, gave a publicity that was almost modern to the antics of the royal dukes.*[39]

In any other European country expenditure such as that of the Prince of Wales on Carlton House, and later at Brighton, would have passed virtually unnoticed by all but an inner circle of aristocratic society.[40] As it was, the more his many extravagances were exposed to a brutal and sometimes unjust criticism, the

FIG. 55
Tapered decanter, lead crystal glass,
English, *c.*1780
Height: 28.5 cm

The publication of Sir William Hamilton's collection of Greek pottery in 1768 spawned the development of classical shapes like this, with its gentle flowing curves and inward taper on the base. OLD BROWN AND GOOD COMPANY seems a homely motto for a decanter embellished with neoclassical swags and garlands, but it was probably intended for strong ale rather than wine.

FIG. 56
Wine glass, diamond-cut lead crystal,
English, *c.*1808
Height: 14 cm

Like the decanter shown on the right (fig. 57), this wine glass was probably made by Perrin Geddes & Co. for the Prince Regent.

FIG. 57
Decanter, diamond-cut lead crystal,
English, *c.*1810
Height: 26 cm

In contrast to the ale decanter on the left (fig. 55), this one was intended for serving wine. It is likely that it was made by Perrin Geddes & Co. for the Prince Regent. Cut-glass decoration flourished at the end of the Georgian era and this faceting was particularly effective when viewed in candlelight. Most decanters of the period had bulbous bodies, so this majestic straight-sided example is unusual.

more it seemed to encourage his fickleness and indecision. As Lady Sarah Spencer noted:

> *He changes the furniture so very often one can scarcely find time to catch a glimpse of each transient arrangement before it is all turned out for some other.*[41]

For a prince to be spending money on furnishings and decorative arts could be justified as a legitimate investment, but his passion for lavish parties and fêtes weighed heavily on a people burdened by repressive Corn Laws and ever-increasing taxation. It is often stated that the Prince's entertainments were unmatched by those of his contemporaries, but this does not seem to have been the case. Many of the 4,000 pieces of silver, for example, in the so-called 'Grand Service' that Rundell, Bridge & Rundell supplied and repaired in 1811 had their origins in samples provided for other clients.[42]

Having been given Carlton House as a coming-of-age present in August 1783, the Prince of Wales first turned, as a stop-gap, to Sir William Chambers, who put the house in order. During that winter, just after his secret marriage to Mrs Fitzherbert, the Prince purchased from William Duesbury a set of porcelain intended for the dining room table. The order included biscuit figures of classical deities, presumably copying the sugar figures of an earlier generation, and also a dessert service decorated with roses and a rich mosaic border.[43] The set comprised forty-eight plates, twenty-nine comports of different forms (two were heart-shaped) and a pair of covered cream bowls with stands and spoons. Four 'double ice pails' in the same style were added a little later, together with a pair of quart 'Prince' glass decanters with four rings in the neck.[44] By March of 1784 the house was ready for its first Grand Ball and the Prince hired in a further twenty-one biscuit groups and forty-eight figures to complement his existing set.[45]

It is not known exactly how these figures were displayed on the Prince's dining table, but by 1794 they were being supplemented with 'ornaments for the dessert frames, parterres, coloured marble dust, frost, flowers and balustrades', supplied by the London-based toyman Louis-Framant Catherine.[46] It seems likely therefore that the dining room table was intended as an evocation of an arcadian garden, perhaps drawing upon mid-eighteenth century French texts for its inspiration.[47] We know that the Prince did have a great admiration for all things French – his collection of Sèvres porcelain, for example, is the finest in the world – but he was also a great supporter of the British manufacturers.[48] His purchases of porcelain from the Derby, Worcester, Spode and Copeland, Longport and Wedgwood factories are well documented, but for general supplies of glassware he also favoured English suppliers, such as Hargrave & Co. The more specialized cut-glass wares came from Parker & Perry of Fleet Street, who in 1802 provided:

One elegant oval bason for ice fruit on an oval base superbly cut in rich raised waves the bason 16 inches in length with V cut rich of diamonds waves etc the cover imperial star deep scallops and silver gilt handles.	*35. 0.0*
Making moulds (6 oval metal ones)	*12.10.0*
For 'do' turning wood patterns etc.[49]	

These outgoings were quite modest compared to later purchases during the Regency (1811–20), but there is also other evidence of constraint. For general use at the table, for example, the linen draper Harry Barker in 1805 supplied four dozen huckaback tablecloths (at £2 each), two dozen diaper cloths and twelve dozen long towels decorated with coronets, letters and figures.[50] On special occasions, however, the Prince did demand a superior standard, and he turned to the famed Irish linen-weavers for cloth of the requisite quality. The most significant purchases of linen were made during the years 1805–10, when he received various sets of superfine damask table linen woven by J.W. Coulson of Lisburn: twelve tablecloths of different sizes, 'slips for ends and sides of table cloths', 188 dinner napkins and forty-two dessert napkins, all woven with crests, garter star and wreaths of oak, laurel and shamrock (see fig. 54). For these he paid the extraordinary sum of £2,166.3s.0d; the cheapest set was a single eight-yard tablecloth and forty-eight napkins costing £174.6s.0d.[51] If we compare this cost with a large extending mahogany dining table that Robert Butler designed and supplied for £140.0s.0d in 1811, clearly, in the hierarchy of dining room display, the mahogany table was now playing a secondary role.[52]

This period just prior to the Regency was a positive frenzy of anticipation. Building projects at Carlton House were now under the direction of the dilettante and writer Walsh Porter, who had been commissioned to sweep away much of Henry Holland's previous works.[53] The decoration of Dominique Daguerre was being displaced by a more exotic mix of Gothic, Egyptian and chinoiserie styles. On the dining table it was Chinese fantasy that prevailed (for the moment). The German artist Benjim Zobel painted nine (lacquered) dessert frames for the Prince in 1806,[54] whilst the toyman Catherine supplied Chinese baldachinos, bridges, pavilions, trees and gilded gates to ornament them.[55] The following year, however, the Prince began adding to his collection of Sèvres porcelain through the London dealer, Robert Fogg, who provided '2 Seve Plateaux' at a cost of £105.5s.0d.[56] On completion of the new Gothic conservatory at Carlton House, he bought in a large selection of 'rich cut' water glasses, liquors, wines, pint decanters and 'crafts' (carafes) just in time for the Christmas celebrations of 1809.[57]

It was also during this period that the Prince conceived the idea of the so-called 'Grand Service' of silver and silver gilt to be fashioned by the royal goldsmiths, Rundell, Bridge & Rundell. On 3 May 1806 Farrington wrote in his diary: 'The Prince has also ordered plate from Rundells to the amount of £70,000 among which are articles which can never be required to be used.'[58]

Whilst Farrington was certainly right about the final costs, a study of the invoice does not bear out his assumption that some pieces would not be needed. Some, of course, were meant for show on the tiered sideboard, but the great majority were for use on the dining room table.[59] Many of his 'Grand Service' pieces have been fully described elsewhere;[60] however, others acquired by the Prince but no longer surviving in the Royal Collection offer us a glimpse of the Prince's passion for pageantry. An older plateau,[61] for example, was substantially altered and gilded:

> *A very large and superb chased silver border to a plateau, device, trophies of war, flags and festoons of drapery, with chased armour of Edward the Black Prince.*
>
> *1034 oz 6 dcts fashn 10/6d.*[62]

Also purchased were two 'very large and superb ornaments for the centre', decorated with piping fawns and dancing nymphs supporting 'baskets and linings for flowers', plus two smaller versions for each end of the table. This is seemingly one of the earliest references to specific stands for natural flower decoration being provided on the English dining table.[63] Taking the whole invoice into account, and including for the reconditioning of over 500 older pieces, the Prince could now provide a complete table setting for 150 people in silver and silver gilt, for both courses.

In January 1811, some two weeks before his installation as Regent, he acquired through the assistance of Robert Fogg an extraordinary blue and gold ground dessert service that had been personally commissioned from the

FIG. 58
One of a pair of candelabra, silver-gilt, by Smith & Sharp, 1811/12 (part of a group of twenty-four made in stages, 1804–12)
Height: 64 cm

While the rest of the population suffered as a result of blockades, the privations caused by the Napoleonic Wars failed to restrain the Prince Regent's taste for magnificence. According to the Royal Archives, in 1811 he purchased from Rundell's '12 large richly chased candelabra for the table on tripod feet, with chased trumpet branches and centre'. He was billed for £2,294.0s.3d, plus an additional £577.4s.0d for gilding and engraving. The glamour of the spoils from Napoleon's Egyptian campaign and an antiquarian interest in the exotic motifs of ancient Egypt permeated the fine and decorative arts at this time, as the Pharaonic head at the top of the stem attests.

FIG. 59
Sauceboat and stand, silver-gilt
Smith & Scott, 1804/5
Height: 23 cm

The style of Anglo-French cuisine favoured by the Regent called for a large number of sauces to add relish to the principal dishes, and their preparation required not only skill but also a fine-tuned palate. Cooks were advised to keep their stomachs from strong liquors and their noses free of snuff. The Grand Service included 'twelve sauce tureens, with covers & stands to suit' to accommodate these essential accompaniments to boiled, stewed and braised meats and fish. The design not only draws inspiration from Pharaonic Egypt, but also incorporates decorative elements from the engravings of Percier and Fontaine (1801).

Sèvres factory by Louis XVI in 1783.[64] This lavish assembly, some twenty-three years in the making, was perfectly fitting for a future King of England, and its strong associations with a royal family he so admired must have made the purchase even more pleasing.

It has been suggested that this dessert service was never used by George IV, but shortly after the acquisition of the set Robert Fogg supplied a matching 'Seve Porcelain Plateaux – fine Blue and Gold ground and figures',[65] which suggests that the Prince was considering his dining table layout just as much as his cabinet display. With this in mind, one can imagine its first usage being at Carlton House on 19 June 1811, when the Prince Regent gave a spectacular celebration party for 2,000 and where the principal guest was the exiled Louis XVIII of France. The *Annual Register* was effusive in its praise of this occasion:

> *The appearance of the* [Gothic] *conservatory was truly striking and brilliant – The upper end was a circular buffet on which stood a variety of the most gorgeous plate. Supplied, as indeed all the tables were, with every attainable delicacy and luxury – embellished by all the art and skill of the confectioner, with the emblematical devices of every conceivable description.* [At the other end] *In front of the Regent's seat there was a circular bason of water, with an enriched temple in the centre of it,*[54] *from whence there was a meandering stream to the bottom of the table bordered with green banks. Three or four fantastic bridges were thrown over it,*[67] *one of them with a small tower upon it, which gave the stream a picturesque appearance. It contained also a number of gold and silver fish.*

Although gilded fish made out of blancmange, swimming in 'water' made of jelly, were popular table decorations at this time, the Prince Regent actually used live fish on this occasion, which caused much comment among the guests.[68]

Sadly there is no record of what food was brought to the table, but a Carlton House menu book, covering the period 6 April 1812 to June 1820, gives an excellent overview of the Regent's preferences and suggests a likely composition of the food on offer.[69] This record, which deserves further detailed study, reveals a surprising consistency in the menus (be they written out in French or in English) even during the residency of the famous French chef Carème.[70] It was possibly this lack of adventure and appreciation, as much as the English climate, that prompted Carème's return to the Continent after only two years in office.

BILL OF FARE

Soup à la Reine
Rice and Chickens (soup)
Julliene
Vermicilly (soup with fowls)
2 Chickens
1 Guinea fowls
1 Capon
2 Minced Pullets
2 Chickens with cauliflower
2 Fricassee of Chickens
1 Lamb Cutlets
1 Sweet Breads
2 Fillets of Capon Brigaree
Pease
Spinnage
Asparagus
Potatoes

COLD
2 Hams
2 Tongues
2 Dabs
2 Capon Pies
1 Capon Aspick
1 Meal cake and ribs of lamb

16 ENTREES
Fricassee of Chickens
Chicken Aspick
Fricandaeux
Sho [house] Lamb
Fillets of Pullets with Truffles
Fillets of Soles
Lobster Salad

Prince Regent's Table, 1 June 1813

Crayfish
Marmalade of Chickens
Gallantine
Truffles

16 ENTREMETS
Strawberry Jelly
Wine Jelly
Noyeau Jelly
Orange Jelly
Cream of Mariskino
Blancmange
Cream of Coffee
Cream of Orange Flowers
4 Jellies

Pastry by Mr le Clerc
8 Gross Pieces
1 Savory Cake à la Chantilly
1 German 'do'
2 Baskets garnished
1 Cherry Tartlet
1 Cherry Tart
1 Vol au Vent of currants
1 Choux Grelley
1 Genevoise

Confectionery by Mr Benois
A frame ornamented with:
3 Triffles
24 Ornaments with bonbons and biscuits
20 Dishes of fruits
8 Ices
8 Compotes

The transcription of a manuscript dinner menu reproduced here gives a good indication of the Regent's preferred dishes. The total quantities consumed were also given, together with the list of wines: 'Port 17, Sherry 24, Claret 3, Madeira 6, Champin 2, Brandy 2.'[71]

Unfortunately, we do not know how many guests were at this party or how the seventeen tables were laid out, but luckily Jean-Baptiste Watier, the Clerk-Comptroller of the kitchen, was more detailed in his record of the King's Coronation Banquet at Westminster Hall on 19 July 1821. In a handsome bound volume he lists all the provisions and shows table plans for the 2,000 guests, all carefully drawn out and numbered.[72] The location of objects such as ice pails, salts and plateaux are all identified, which makes it interesting to compare these plans with paintings said to depict the occasion (see fig. 53).

Clearly the King's table is laid out and served *à la Française*. Both he and the six other princes had a choice of twenty dishes during the first course, twenty-two in the second and thirty-one for dessert. But this is not to say that all the dishes were sampled. For example, Lord Denbigh noted in his diary:

> *The King was very gracious to me at the banquet and called me to him. He gave me his hand to kiss and desired me to stand opposite to him at table and help him to some turtle soup to which I also helped the rest of the Royal Dukes ... I also helped a dish of quails, and carved a slice out of a capon for the Duke of York. I had not a very arduous office as the Royal Dukes had dined previously. Lord Colchester was my assistant carver and cut up a pineapple weighing eleven pounds.*[73]

When the King retired at about 7.30 pm, the rest of the dignitaries, who had eaten nothing since breakfast, set upon the 3,903 hot and cold dishes with relish as wives and children gazed on in desperation from the rows of seats above.[74]

To make operations easier, the city chef had laid up all the other tables with cold dishes on display and the hot soups, fishes, vegetables, joints and sauces served from adjoining sideboards. A similar presentation prevailed when the King made a hugely successful state visit to Scotland the following year. The City of Edinburgh put on a splendid banquet for 300 on 24 August 1822, which the historian Robert Murdie described in great detail.[75]

Once again the King had over twenty dishes on offer for first and second courses, but he limited himself to 'turtle and grouse soups, stewed carp and venison in the first course; and in the second course, of grouse and apricot tart. During dinner he drank moselle and a little champagne, and claret during the rest of the evening. He made use of glasses 200 years old, of a very massive and antique form, which had been furnished for his table by Sir Walter Scott.'[76]

For dessert the King sampled the peaches, pineapples and other fruits on offer and was 'well pleased' with the water ices, cream ices and orange chips provided by the confectioner, Mr Davidson.[77] After dinner the Lord Provost of Edinburgh began a series of toasts that were to become the stuff of legend. The King, by this time a gouty old man of sixty, withdrew gracefully after the fifth toast, but the company continued on for another forty, all to be given, as was the military custom, 'three times three'.[78] The question of how the 300 guests managed to keep their glasses full and their minds composed for forty-five toasts is not addressed in the account, but it is highly likely that they were serving themselves from decanters on the table.

It is around this time that mobile structures for wine on the table were being proposed and typically the King was quick to adopt this novel mode of 'transport'. In July of 1826 an order was immediately placed with the Birmingham silversmith Edward Thomason, who supplied:

> *Two carriages with complete axles to move and turn conveniently upon the dinner table – each capable of holding two decanters – made of silver, stamped at His Majesty's Assay Office and rich gilt in ormolu.*[79]

The timing of this invention could not have been better; it is not hard to imagine the convenience it provided for a King more and more restricted in his movements by stomach pains and gout. By 1830 the extravagant lifestyle was catching up with him, although his mode of living was still 'really beyond belief'.[80] For breakfast, for example, on 9 April, Lord Wellington said he had:

> *Two pigeons and three beef steaks, three parts of a bottle of mozelle, a glass of dry champagne, two glasses of port, a glass of brandy.*[81]

Despite his dependency on laudanum, the King died in great pain on 25 June 1830. Wellington's eulogy in the House of Lords praised George IV as a 'most magnificent patron of the arts in this country, and in the world'. He also noted:

> *...the most extraordinary compound of talent, wit, buffoonery, obstinacy and good feeling – in short a medley of the most opposite qualities, with a great preponderance of good – that I ever saw in any character in my life.*[82]

FIG. 60
Tureen, cover and stand, silver-gilt
Paul Storr, 1802/3
Height: 45 cm

Turtle soup, usually followed by *ponche à la Régence*, was George's favourite dish, so it may frequently have been served from this magnificent tureen. According to Rundell's bill of 1811, four 'very large and elegant richly chased' tureens and four identical but smaller ones were first supplied ungilded, for a total sum of £4,498.13s.9d. At large state dinners a variety of soups and ragouts were served amongst the *grosses entrées*, so all eight of these tureens may well have been on the table at the opening of the meal, those containing soup subsequently being replaced by the removes.

Storr's tureen incorporates a welter of design motifs and symbols from both the neoclassical and the Egyptian styles – a shamelessly adulatory tribute to the magnificence of the Regent's palace at Carlton House. The handles, in the form of a winged and crowned Artemis of Ephesus emerging from a cornucopia, symbolize victory, power and abundance.

FIG. 61
Harold Gilman (1876–1919), *Mrs Mounter at the Breakfast Table*, 1917
Oil on canvas, 61 × 40 cm

The singularly unperceptive critic who sneered at the 'shabby gentility' of Harold Gilman's lodgings in Fitzrovia could not have been more wrong. Mrs Mounter and her household were neither shabby nor genteel. This portrait is an affectionate tribute to the care with which Gilman's landlady presided over his life in the years before his second marriage. Other versions of this portrait, and some interiors, show Mrs Mounter among her things, a personality at one with her surroundings, comfortably and securely working class. These traits are apparent even in a sketch of Mrs Mounter surveying the confusion of Gilman's studio with a grim benevolence. Here her breakfast table is laid with strong, no-nonsense crockery: the big white cups are solid and homely, and the 'Brown Betty' teapot was already set to become a working-class icon among the artists and students of Gilman's circle.

CHAPTER 3

The Great British Breakfast

THE STANDARD breakfast fry-up of every modern British hotel and motorway café seems almost insubstantial when compared with its protein-rich Tudor equivalent. Even the dietary restrictions of sixteenth-century fast days failed to prevent breakfast from being a hefty meal, at least for the rich. During Lent of 1512 the Earl and Countess of Northumberland breakfasted daily on 'a loaf of bread, two manchetts, a quart of ale, a quart of wine, two pieces of salt fish, six bawned herrings, four white herrings, or a dish of sprats'. On days when meat was permissible, the fish was replaced with 'half a chyne of mutton, or a chyne of boiled beef', usually left over from the previous day and served cold. A chyne was the saddle made up of a section of the animal's spine with three or four ribs on each side, an extraordinarily generous cut of meat for an early morning meal.[1] Although some members of important households preferred lighter, meatless breakfasts, it was still customary to consume copious quantities of household ale, which was safer to drink than water. Queen Elizabeth seems to have preferred this plainer style of breakfasting on little more than brown and white bread and beer. On one occasion, in 1576, she was served for breakfast 'cheate and manchett 6d, ale and beare 3 and half d, wine one pint, 7d'.[2]

While the well-heeled started their day with substantial helpings of beer, bread and beef, humbler families breakfasted on pottage made with the local cereal: wheat in the south, oats and barley in the north. Porridge, hasty pudding, crowdi, washbrew, girdbrew, flummery and poddish, all regional variants of oatmeal potage, were the chief foods of the labouring man, not only for breakfast but for supper too. According to Gervase Markham, who considered oatmeal to be 'the very Crowne of the Housewifes garland', early seventeenth-century seafarers enjoyed a buttery version of groat porridge called loblolly.[3]

Spice bread became a feature of the gentry breakfast during the seventeenth century, but the biggest change to the meal came after the introduction of tea in the second half of the century, when the rich and fashionable, at least, started to move away from ale and took to the new oriental beverage as the ideal drink

FIG. 62
Joseph Michael Gandy (1771–1843),
The Breakfast Room at 12 Lincoln's Inn Fields, c.1798
Watercolour on paper, 64.5 × 65 cm

The Soane family had been living in their new house in Lincoln's Inn Fields for four years when Joseph Gandy, one of Soane's pupils, recorded them at breakfast in the newly built breakfast room. We see a calm and relatively uncluttered room, with Soane's ingenious use of mirrors and reflections maximizing the light filtering in through the array of potted plants that concealed the bricks and mortar of a typical London back yard. A placid, conventional breakfast of tea or coffee with toast and bread and butter is taking place in a manically progressive environment. Soane filled his house with ultra-modern concepts: water closets, central heating, the most up-to-date kitchen equipment. He also embellished it with concealed lighting, unexpected vistas through unimaginable spaces to unbelievable objects, paintings lurking in impossible recesses, chunks of antique marble cheek-by-jowl with mouldering medieval remains, cabinets of precious stones, and niches for the display of coins, cameos and curiosities. But within this idiosyncratic environment the Soanes lived the typical domestic life of a young professional couple – Mrs Soane, adored and revered by her household staff and irascible husband, tells in her diary and household accounts of shopping, dressmaking, payments to tradesmen, organized trips to the theatre and dinner parties with friends.

to start the day. By the 1730s for most people breakfast had become a lighter meal of bread and butter, with tea universally accepted by both rich and poor. The recollections of those old enough to remember the beef and beer breakfasts of the age before tea were regarded with some curiosity. In an entry in *Applebie's Journal* for September 1731 we are informed:

> *An old gentleman near ninety, who has a florid and vigorous constitution tells us the difference between the manners of the present age, and that in which he spent his youth. With regard to eating in his time, Breakfast consisted of good hams, cold sirloin, and good beer, succeeded with wholesome exercise, which sent them home hungry and ready for dinner.*[4]

By the end of the eighteenth century the universal adoption of tea and white bread and butter at breakfast by the poor of southern England was being criticized by some prominent members of the medical profession. Against a background of grain shortages and high bread prices, the Scottish physician William Buchan, in his best-selling family encyclopaedia *Domestic Medicine* (1783), warned his readers against the expense and dangers to health of such a diet (see also pp.117–19). Like Markham, he was an apologist for oats and advocated the porridge of his native Scotland as the most suitable breakfast food for the labouring classes. Despite the terrible shortages of the 1790s, the English aversion to any grain other than wheat meant that this sensible advice went unheeded. In the 1803 edition of his work he sadly remarked of oats: 'I wish the horses in England devoured a smaller quantity of that grain and the people more.' He was particularly concerned about the diet of children:

> *Children are seldom well, unless when their bodies are gently open. But this is more likely to be the case when fed on oatmeal and milk, than when their bodies are crammed with a starchy substance made of the finest flour; yet this in England is the common food of children. I have seen an infant stuffed four or five times a-day with this kind of food. There needs no conjuror to tell the consequence.*[5]

These arguments against refined foods such as white bread, and the consequent adoption of whole grains, particularly oats, were to surface again in the 1960s, when muesli began to appear on the table of the health-conscious breakfaster.

One of the most interesting accounts of an English breakfast in a great eighteenth-century country house was given by the French traveller François de Rochefoucauld, who in 1784 stayed at Euston Hall, the home of the Duke of Grafton:

> *It is usual throughout England to breakfast together, in the same way that we come together in France for dinner or supper. The favourite time for breakfast is nine o'clock, and already the ladies' hair is done and they are dressed for the most part for the rest of the day. Breakfast consists of tea and various forms of bread and butter. In rich men's houses, you have coffee, chocolate, etc. Invariably, the newspapers are on the table, and those who wish, read them during breakfast, so, usually, conversation is not very lively. At 10.30 or 11, everyone goes his own way, to hunt, or fish, or go walking. In all that, one does more or less as one pleases, and so it's very agreeable. That is how it is until 4 o' clock, but at 4 o' clock precisely, one must be in the drawing-room, and there the formalities are more than we are accustomed to in France. This sudden change of manners is astonishing; I was much struck by it. In the morning you come down in your top boots and a dirty old coat, sit where you like, behave in the room exactly as if you were alone, nobody notices you, nothing could be more relaxed. But, in the evening, you must be very proper, unless you have just that moment arrived. One observes an uncomfortable politeness; strangers go in first to dinner and sit near the lady of the house; they are seated in order of seniority with the most rigid etiquette; so much so that, for the first few days, I was inclined to believe they were doing it for a joke.*[6]

It is interesting to note the early appearance here of that indispensable accoutrement at the modern breakfast table, the morning newspaper (figs 62, 65 & 68). In the 1820s a number of specialized journals, bearing such titles as *Dry Toast* and *The Déjeuné; or, Companion for the Breakfast Table*, were published specifically for breakfast-time reading, but they proved a shortlived novelty.[7] Sophisticated Mayfair breakfasters at this time may have perused one of these modish periodicals while they enjoyed a turtulong with their morning tea or coffee. The breakfast turtulong was a bagel-like roll, popularized by the Italian confectioner Domenico Negri, who had a shop in Berkeley Square in the 1760s. Like *Dry Toast* and the other breakfast periodicals, it never really caught on beyond aristocratic circles.[8]

FIG. 63
Mary Ellen Best (1809–91),
Dining Room at Langton Hall, Family at Breakfast, c.1832–4
Watercolour on paper, 21 × 33 cm

The interest taken by Mary Ellen Best in the lives and surroundings of her family and friends was recorded in her thousands of watercolour sketches. This scene of her maternal grandmother and uncle and aunts at breakfast at their home just outside York is typical of the genteel lifestyle of the comfortably-off but unpretentious friends and relatives that Mary Ellen visited. Their ample breakfast is all there on the table, rather than being served from a sideboard. It seems to consist mainly of those worthy Yorkshire buns, teacakes and muffins that did so much to keep out the cold, while a tea urn and coffee pot tell us what beverages were drunk.

When Mary Ellen married and settled in Germany, she appears to have enjoyed her Bavarian in-laws' warm stoves and ethereal pastries. The many sketches she made depicting domestic life in that country bear witness to the fact that she retained the same enthusiasm for kitchens and bright, cheerful interiors that she had displayed as a girl.

By the reign of Victoria the enormous wealth generated by both the Empire and the manufacturing industries had resulted in the creation of a huge new town-based middle class, who aspired to imitate the lifestyle of their social superiors. Unlike the relaxed simple affairs of the previous century, breakfasts in the houses of the wealthy were frequently formal meals of great complexity, with a huge range of dishes on offer. Contemporary cookery authors attempted to promote this elaborate style of country house breakfast in their books, most of which were aimed at middle-class households. In the following essay Eileen White demonstrates that ambitious breakfasts, were an ideal hardly ever realized outside the breakfast rooms of great country houses.

FIG. 64
Roderic Barrett (b.1920),
Family Breakfast, 1954
Oil on canvas, 90 × 75 cm

'Dangerous-looking children; dangerous-looking furniture,' commented a life-long admirer of Barrett's affectionately disturbing vision of domestic life. Here a post-Festival of Britain nuclear family struggles to enjoy its liberation from stifling Victorian conventions of behaviour and the suffocating norms of middle-class interior decoration. Noise predominates. Cornflakes (muesli was barely a glint in progressive eyes) crunch underfoot on the terrazzo flooring. Mugs and spoons clatter across the fashionable tiled table-top with its neat matt black steel trim, crisp edges and sharp corners. The 'Good Enough Parents', wan and green with exhaustion, pay heed, as they have been encouraged to do by Spock and Winnecot, to the exhortations of their vociferous brood. But there is some consolation in the fresh, clean lines of the tableware and the shiny cutlery. A bright modern interior in a brave new world, a moment of innocent optimism between the austerity of the post-war years and the nightmare threat of nuclear wars to come. Packaged cereals, claiming to contain everything needed for a brisk start to the day, liberated a servantless family from the tyranny of the cooked breakfast and provided a window of opportunity for virtuous raw fruit and yoghurt, Grape Nuts and All Bran. The exciting new 'instant' coffee was made direct in the mug and the rasp of grit and crumbs on the smeared tabletop was an acceptable alternative to the laundered napery and conventional table settings of earlier generations.

The Ideal and the Real

BREAKFAST AT THE DAWN OF THE TWENTIETH CENTURY

BREAKFAST is Britain's most famous culinary contribution, yet a cooked meal of bacon, eggs and sausages to start the day is perhaps an ideal more dreamed of than achieved as we move into the twenty-first century. The elements of the traditional British breakfast can be traced back several hundred years. Even in the early seventeeth century porridge was a long-established breakfast for farmworkers, for whom a pot of it would be left simmering by the fire,[9] and the combination of bacon and eggs was well entrenched by the time Sir Kenelm Digby was compiling his notes in the middle of the century. He also suggested a fine oatmeal or barley porridge, along with new-laid eggs.[10] We know that Oliver Cromwell and his wife enjoyed sausages, including some made from bonemarrow and almonds as opposed to the now ubiquitous pork.[11] In grand country houses the morning meal would have been taken at a relaxed pace with people coming and going as it suited them, the relatively new beverages of tea, coffee and chocolate adding to their enjoyment.

Breakfast had come a long way from the beef and ale consumed in large Tudor households,[12] but it was in the Victorian and Edwardian eras that it was to rise to its greatest glory. Books dedicated exclusively to the topic – from *The Breakfast Book* (1865) to Florence B. Jack's *Breakfast and Savoury Dishes* (1903) and beyond – as well as sections on breakfast fare in more general cookery books, provided an astonishing variety of options for the first meal of the day that helped fuel Victorian industrial and colonial expansion.

Cookery books of the 1860s seem to have taken the morning meal more for granted, with *The Breakfast Book* posing the question 'What can we have for breakfast?' as the starting point for giving a long list of permissible items.[13] It also defined different types of breakfast. The family breakfast could be made up of a variety of hors d'œuvres or by-dishes, hot or cold, while *déjeuner à la fourchette* was served in courses, similar to a dinner. A further alternative was the cold collation, for which, it was stated, 'almost all recherché things are proper' (a reminder that one of the origins of breakfast fare was the use of food left over from the day before). However, the most common type of breakfast was the ambigue, consisting of a heterogeneous collection of items all placed on the table at once: 'Our everyday breakfasts are in a small way served *en ambigu*, inasmuch as broiled fish, cold pasties, devilled bones, boiled eggs, cold ham, etc, all appear together.'[14]

The first edition of Mrs Beeton's *Book of Household Management* (1861) devoted less space to 'the comfortable meal called breakfast' than some of the later editions were to do, but it did summarize the typical fare to be found throughout the Victorian period. Cold meats, nicely garnished, were to be placed on the sideboard, including collared and potted meat or fish, cold game or poultry, meat pies, ham and tongue. Suggestions for hot dishes included broiled fish, mutton chops, rump steak, kidneys, sausages, rashers of bacon, ham, poached eggs, omelettes and boiled eggs. Muffins, toast, butter, marmalade and the like were the regular accompaniments, and 'when convenient, a nicely-arranged dish of fruit'.[15]

Subsequent editions contained expanded sections on each meal of the day, including breakfast. Detailed instructions were given for laying the table, garnishing the dishes and setting out the tea and coffee. The 1880 edition gave a brief description of the 'cold joints, hot nick-nacks and potted meats' that made up the meal, adding sardines and anchovies to the suggested fish, as well as an innovation – Australian tinned meat. Watercress was recommended 'from a sanitary point of view'.[16]

Frederick Bishop, in *The Wife's Own Book of Cookery* (1862), was also concerned with the laying out of a table for breakfast, while the food and drink he proposed included a selection of hot and cold meat and fish, devilled poultry, cold meat pies and patties, eggs, kidneys and ham, fruit (ripe or preserved), and tea, coffee, toast and rolls.[17] Twenty-five years later Major L..., in his *Breakfasts, Luncheons, and Ball Suppers* (1887), declared that a good country house breakfast should offer fish, poultry or game, sausages, mutton cutlets or beef fillets, omelettes and eggs, and cold ham, tongue, meat pies or galantines, with spiced beef in winter, as well as bread, jam, marmalade and fruit.[18]

Although *The Breakfast Book* lists eggs and bacon among 'Things Most Commonly Served for Family Breakfasts', its alphabetically arranged recipes also include anchovies, beef steaks, caviare, mutton chops, pork cutlets, red or white herrings, sheep's tongues ('Though certainly not a recherché comestible, sheeps tongues have their admirers...'), shrimps, prawns, crayfish and smoked haddock. The second chapter gives instructions for made dishes that can be quickly prepared, such as curries and rissoles, while later ones describe savoury pies, galantines and cold meat in jelly, and collared, pickled and potted meat.

There was, then, a great variety of recommendations, both elaborate and simple, as to how to prepare and serve the ideal breakfast. But the very repetition by cookery writers of 'ideal' versions of the meal leads one to wonder how many people actually took up their suggestions. Given, too, that so many of the cookery books stress the need for greater variety, to what extent do they reveal the *real* breakfasts eaten by ordinary people at the beginning of the nineteenth century? One source in particular helps us find out, since it presents the results of a study into the menus of various families, noted for a week at a time, which can be compared with the ideals put forward in the contemporary cookery books.

It was around 1900 that B. Seebohm Rowntree carried out his research for *Poverty: A Study of Town Life*, first published in 1901, by looking in detail at the living conditions in 'a single typical town', namely York. In chapter VIII of his book he set out the family budgets and diets of twenty-four families. The majority of these – fourteen – fell into the poorest class, categorized as households with an income of less than 26 shillings per week. The families in class 2, of which there were four, were those receiving a weekly wage of up to about 40 shillings. As a control, class 3 was made up of six families of the servant-keeping class, although here only the diets were presented, no information on income and expenditure being revealed.

In every case the family recorded in detail all their meals over a certain period of time, then Rowntree selected a typical week to use as an example. The size of each family was stated, but Rowntree's tables do not indicate how much individual family members ate of the food provided; presumably the father would have been given the largest share. In family 12 of class 1 the man of the house sometimes took his breakfast to work with him; his wife explained that, whilst she and her four children had no meat in the morning, her husband 'must have a bit of bacon to take with him for his breakfast, or else the others would talk so'.[19]

Common to the breakfasts in all three classes was bread in various forms: white, brown and teacakes. Sometimes it was taken in the form of toast, sometimes toast and bread appeared together on the table, and sometimes there was both white and brown. In addition there are ten references to cake, scones or

FIG. 65
Benjamin Robert Haydon (1786–1846), *An Unexpected Visitor*, c.1835
Oil on canvas, 76 × 64 cm

Benjamin Robert Haydon's Napoleonic sense of his own destiny as a painter in the grand manner was never realized. Even his prodigious energies, wit and charm failed to persuade the public to buy his huge history paintings and he was forced instead to eke out a living by creating small domestic scenes such as *An Unexpected Visitor*. He hated having to paint this kind of popular 'potboiler' and failed to appreciate that applying his skills to scenes from everyday life might have brought him greater acclaim and wealth than his ill-conceived ambitious projects. This somewhat ambivalent scene reflects all too clearly his own messy financial affairs and professional life. The grimace with which the dissolute young man greets the hollow bonhomie of the bailiff is all too true to life. By the time the painting was completed Haydon had been arrested for debt several times. He himself commented: 'I am sorry to say that my ambition ever dwindles unless kept alive by risk of ruin.'

Here we see a characteristic day of reckoning, where the cost of a wild night out comes home to roost unexpectedly early. Meanwhile the weak tea and soft-boiled eggs in their fashionable egg cups jostle for position on the table with the decanter and glasses of the night before. A neglected oil lamp gutters on the mantelpiece as a sickly morning light falls on the crumpled bonnet discarded on a chair, and the empty purse, waved provocatively at the visitor, proclaims a defiance in the face of, if not ruin, then a thoroughly unpleasant morning after.

shortbread. By far the most popular drink was tea, mentioned 155 times in the 182 menus provided, while coffee received 37 mentions. An alternative drink was milk, occasionally heated. Butter was recorded by all the families, with dripping used on ten occasions by class 1 households. Bacon was the other typical item, appearing on most breakfast menus at least once or twice a week. Ham appeared at two class 2 breakfasts, and in class 3 twice for family 20 and three times for family 21. Sausages were mentioned only three times, for one class 1 family and two families in class 2 (one of which mentioned specifically 'tomato sausages'). All these examples refer to a Sunday. Eggs were eaten by two of the class 1 families, on one day of the week only, and by two of the class 2 families, on four days. Most families in class 3 had eggs 1–6 days a week. Porridge was eaten occasionally by two class 1 families, one class 2 family and three in class 3.

The breakfast-time eating habits detailed by the wealthier class 3 families in Rowntree's study indicate that the recommendations of the cookery writers were not made entirely in vain. Also, the very fact that some of the books considered here ran to several editions over a period of years demonstrates that there must have been a continuing demand for both general and specialized volumes presenting ideas for the ideal breakfast. On the other hand, reality (on the evidence of Rowntree's study) proves that in practice most families restricted themselves to a much more limited menu than the extensive fare described in the books.

The concept of bacon and eggs, and perhaps sausages, as the mainstay of the British breakfast, still widespread at the close of the twentieth century, was prevalent even at the end of the nineteenth. At that time, however, these foods were seen – at least by those who aspired to the ideal breakfasts detailed in the cookery books – as little more than a framework on which to build. Although most cookery writers of the Victorian era would have been aware of the breakfasting habits of poorer sections of the community, such as those revealed in York, this did not deter them from recommending an ever wider variety of foods, even for those on a low budget.

Some ventured a step further to describe the substantial but leisured morning meal of the country house. The table plan reproduced on page 105, taken from an 1892 edition of 'Mrs Beeton', was used as the basis of our reconstruction of just such a grand breakfast (see fig. 66). This can indeed be seen as the ideal at the beginning of the twentieth century – the Great British Breakfast at its most lavish.

Fig. 66
A country house breakfast – re-created after a table plan in Mrs Beeton's *Book of Household Management* (illustrated below)

Although it looks to modern eyes more like a Lord Mayor's feast than a breakfast, this extraordinary assemblage of dishes would have been less trouble to prepare in a well-regulated Victorian kitchen than might at first sight appear. The cold dishes on the sideboard would have been made well in advance and fetched from the larder when required; it was little trouble for the cook to roast a few extra fowls at the range when preparing dinner the previous day. Only the hot dishes on the table would have been cooked fresh immediately before serving, and even these were quick to prepare. However, the setting-up and clearing of the table and the meticulous cleaning of silver, glass and plates would have created an enormous amount of work, making this kind of arrangement feasible only in establishments with a sizeable team of servants.

Mrs Beeton set great store by the use of a tablecloth at breakfast, for 'it exercises a certain moral influence upon the inmates of the house in the degree of care or thought that is bestowed upon it'. The table napkins were to be tastefully folded when first laid on the table, 'although afterwards in ordinary family use they may be put into rings'. In this edition Mrs Beeton illustrated ten different ways of folding a napkin, noting too that breakfast napkins are usually smaller (24 inches) than those used at dinner (29–30 inches). An early Victorian breakfast service of Derby manufacture has been used for this re-creation; the bread and butter plate is to the side of each place setting, with stacks of dinner plates at the end of the table and on the sideboard. There is matching King's pattern cutlery for the cold meats and fruit on display. In the centre is a Victorian flower stand with trumpet vases, holding a summer arrangement of roses and fern. At the front we see a tray for tea and coffee, which is still, as the author points out, the absolute domain of the mistress of the household. 'Larger dining tables may have a separate tray for coffee or chocolate at the other end,' she instructed, but this still had to be serviced by the eldest daughter or another lady 'president'.

The mid-nineteenth century metal equipage is a mixture of silver, Sheffield plate and the newly developed electroplate by Elkington. Products made by these cheaper techniques had a dramatic effect in bringing the cost of heated entrée dishes, for example, within the budget of a middle-class family.

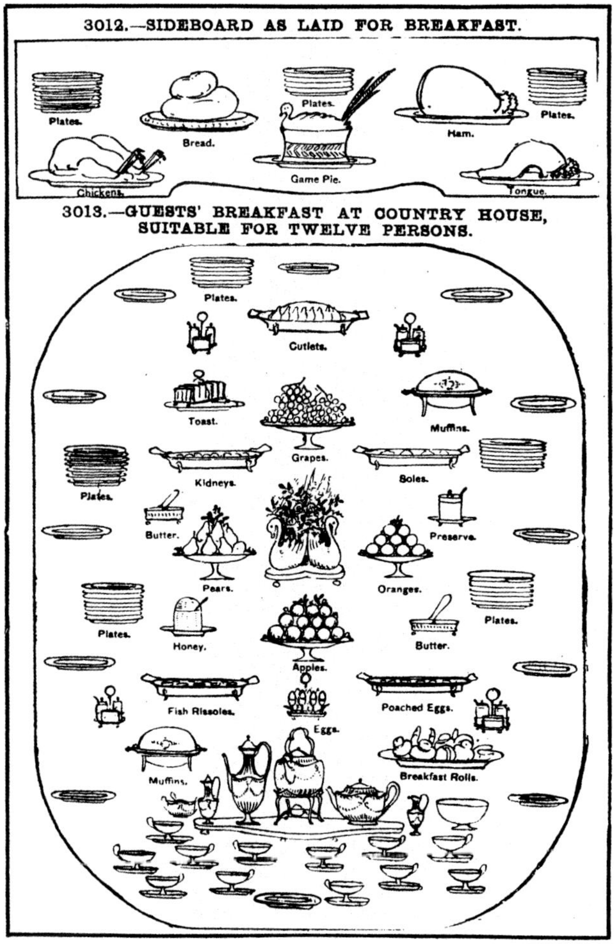

Fig. 67
Breakfast table and sideboard plan from Isabella Beeton's *Book of Household Management* (London 1892), used as the model for the re-creation at Stranger's Hall, Norwich, illustrated opposite

FIG. 68
Charles Spencelayh (1865–1958), *Mother*, 1944
Oil on canvas, 59.5 × 51 cm

Dapper, cheerful, garrulous, chain-smoking Charles Spencelayh was blessed with a carefree childhood, two happy marriages and the modest prosperity of a successful career as a painter of traditional realism. Much to the relief of his patrons and admirers, he ignored the seismic movements in painting and sculpture that transformed the art world during his lifetime. He was content to continue painting in the style he had learnt as an enthusiastic, unrebellious youth at the Royal College of Art, and his subject matter continued to provide the visual equivalent of comfort food for 'Middle England' throughout two world wars and massive social change.

In *Mother*, painted in 1944, the theme of bereavement and loss would have been especially poignant. The scene is a solitary breakfast of bacon and egg, eaten on a rather messily spread cloth on a table in the corner of a living room, on which stands a coffee pot and other treasured but non-matching crockery. The artist has chosen his props with loving care from his collection of bric-à-brac. The day's newspaper lies unfolded on a chair with the change from the weekly payment to the paper boy. What looks like a war map on the front page may help to pin the painting down in time. The morning post, including an airmail letter that could presage bad news or loss, sits unread amidst the remains of breakfast.

But the gaze of the old man is fixed on the portrait of a redoubtable woman in black. The family bible open in front of him, perhaps taken from the unlocked cupboard on the right, may indicate a morbid preoccupation with the anniversary of her death. A sentimental Mother and Child painting or print is hung close to Mother's portrait, and a few fresh flowers have been placed in a vase just below. It is reassuring that the old man, in spite of rationing, has enjoyed a traditional English breakfast before succumbing to his melancholy reflections.

CHAPTER 4

Teatime

FIG. 69
Sir James Gunn (1893–1964),
Conversation Piece at the Royal Lodge, Windsor, 1950
Oil on canvas, 151.1 × 100.3 cm

This intimate glimpse of George VI and Queen Elizabeth (the present Queen Mother) enjoying a homely tea at the Royal Lodge at Windsor with the two princesses, Elizabeth and Margaret Rose, was specially commissioned to help restore the nation's morale during the bleak post-war years. The King, dressed informally, is sitting at ease smoking an ordinary cigarette, a plain box of matches to hand, as he contemplates his daughters, stylish but unostentatious in their New Look frocks. The tea-table, elegant without being extravagant, strikes a similar note of 'making do'. A pretty lace-edged tablecloth and nice tableware compensate for the rather banal tea of plain cake, a few scones, and toast or muffins keeping warm under a domed cover – just the sort of teatime fare with which most ordinary citizens would themselves have been familiar, despite rationing and shortages. This is a clear and heart-warming message that the Royals were sharing, as they had during the Blitz, the same joys and sorrows as the rest of the population.

AS WELL AS being the name of Britain's national hot beverage, 'tea' also signifies a meal or social entertainment that takes place in the afternoon or early evening. Most of us still think in terms of two such meals, afternoon tea and high tea, although neither these terms themselves nor the meals they describe are as commonplace as they used to be. During the nineteenth and early twentieth centuries there were further variations on the theme – for example, 'at home' teas and wedding teas. In some ex-colonial parts of the world the word 'tea' has other shades of meaning. In Jamaica it signifies the opening meal of the day, the equivalent of the British breakfast, while in Australia and New Zealand, where the midday meal is referred to as dinner, tea is a cooked meal served in the evening. What might be called a bar meal in Britain is therefore known in Australian pubs as a 'counter tea'. These differences in nomenclature have occasionally caused embarrassment to visitors who have misunderstood the English definition of the meal, and 'more than one New Zealander has been invited to tea in England and arrived hours too late, the meal finished and the guests gone.'[1]

How did teatime become established as the most quintessentially English, despite being the most recent, of daily meals? Some claim that it came about as a result of a gradual shift in the timing of dinner during the course of the eighteenth century. In the early 1700s the main meal of the day was normally served at about three o'clock in the afternoon, but by the 1800s the fashionable hour for dinner had advanced to six or seven in the evening, creating a need for a light afternoon repast to fill the long gap since breakfast.[2] Anna, wife of the seventh Duke of Bedford (1788–1861), claims to have been the first to introduce a routine afternoon tea with cakes, to counteract 'a sinking feeling' she experienced between lunch and the family's eight o'clock dinner.[3] However, the truth is much more complicated than this and there is compelling evidence to suggest that an upper-class teatime meal emerged well before the Duchess was born. In order to understand the forces that have shaped our teatime as we know it today, it is necessary to examine how tea as a drink came to be absorbed into British domestic life.

Tea was first introduced into Britain in the seventeenth century as an exotic herbal infusion with mild stimulant properties. Pepys first encountered it in 1660, just after it had been made fashionable at court by Catherine of Braganza.[4] It was one of many new plant remedies that entered the country at a time when botanical discoveries from the Far East and the New World were expanding a *materia medica* that had relied for centuries on well-known drugs dating back to the medical authors of antiquity. Merchants, who knew that there was no classical pedigree for tea's remedial properties, were free to make extravagant claims as to the benefits of drinking the new Chinese leaf. The entrepreneurial Thomas Garway skilfully marketed it as a general cure-all in a broadside published in the same year that Pepys drank his first cup:

> *The particular vertues are these: It maketh the Body active and lusty. It helpeth the Headache giddiness and heaviness therof. It removeth the Obstructions of the Spleen ... It (being prepared and drank with Milk and Water) strengtheneth the inward parts, and prevents Consumptions, and powerfully asswageth the pains of the Bowels, or griping of the Guts and Looseness.*[5]

Since Garway was selling it 'from fifteen to fifty shillings the pound', it was very much in his interests to broadcast the miraculous powers of what would have seemed to most, at the time, a rather unattractive drink.

Chocolate, which came into Britain at about the same time, was also marketed aggressively as a medicine before it became established as a social drink. Sex, always the most potent advertising tool, was used unashamedly to popularize it in the early years. Eminent medical men agreed that this 'Indian Nectar' was a powerful aphrodisiac. Henry Stubbes, formerly physician to Lord Windsor in Jamaica, had first-hand experience of the Caribbean folklore surrounding chocolate, as well as valuable interests in His Lordship's cacao plantations. In 1682 he recommended its use above all other sexually stimulating foods:

> *The great Use of Chocolate in Venery, and for Supplying the Testicles with a Balsam, or a Sap, is so ingeniously made out by one of our learned Countrymen already, that I dare not presume to*

FIG. 70
Teapot, slip-cast red stoneware, *c.*1695, probably by J. & D. Elers, Staffordshire
Height: 15 cm

This teapot and a large selection of other redware vessels are recorded in an English country house inventory of 1715, but they may have been in the family's possession a generation before. Most of the other teapots in the collection are Chinese imports, but this example stands out – not only because the modelling seems more assured; on the underside is a square pseudo-Chinese mark that relates to other marks found on late seventeenth-century slipware by the Elers brothers.

> *add any Thing after so accomplished a Pen; though I am of Opinion, that I might treat of the Subject without any Immodesty, or Offence.*[6]

Coffee, the other important new beverage of the seventeenth century, and the first to become popular, was also lauded by some as the great panacea of the age. The London physician William Salmon tells us how, by 'drinking a full quart of Strong coffee at a time', he cured himself of 'a Rheumatick Pain in my Shoulder, which was so vehement I could not so much as lift my Arm or Hand up to my Head, nor put it behind my Back'. He even made a case for using coffee to cure paralysis, an affliction from which he claimed to have suffered since he was a child of eleven: 'This State, and these returns of this dangerous Paralysis, continued with me, till I began to drink Strong Coffee at home, at my own House, which I have done now (1709) for more than ten Years'.[7]

While Salmon was claiming that the powerful stimulant effects of coffee could bring feeling back into his paralysed limbs, others were raising objections that claimed exactly the opposite: 'It causes the Palsie, or a Trembling and Shaking of the Limbs, and is an enemy of the Nerves.' These symptoms, which we would recognize today as those of excessive caffeine consumption, were discounted by Dr Salmon as a myth put about by vintners and innkeepers in a futile attempt to protect their interests from the rapidly growing popularity of coffee houses among the London business community:

> *This is truly nothing but the Vintner's Fable, devised by them against the Use of Coffee, because it so hurts their Trade, or that many hundreds of thousands of Matters and Things are Transacted in a Coffee-House, or over a Dish of Coffee, which would otherwise be done in a Tavern, to the great prejudice of the Wine Office.*[8]

It was almost certainly the vintners who, in the 1670s, put about a rumour that coffee caused impotence, which was summarized in an anonymous broadside entitled the *Women's Petition against Coffee.*[9] Despite their warnings about the drink's threat to masculinity, the vintners and innkeepers eventually lost the 'coffee wars' and the 'abominable, heathenish liquor' rapidly became a popular alternative to ale and claret.

A marked taste among the fashion-conscious for foreign and rare novelties was an important factor in the public acceptance of the three new beverages.

FIG. 71
Pearlware teapot painted in enamel colours and decorated with flower sprays on the reverse, probably made by the Leeds Pottery, *c.*1800–5
Height: 14.1 cm

The pot is decorated with the inscription:

God give us grace to drink
Our tea with bread & butter plenty
With sugar store & water more
to fill the pot when empty

Painted on a teapot of plain material with otherwise simple decoration, this verse supports the claim that – as well as being a fashionable beverage in its own right – by the 1800s at the lower end of the social scale tea was accompanied by a more substantial, satisfying meal which (at the very least) included copious amounts of bread and butter.

FIG. 73
Tea canister, slip-cast red stoneware, Yixing, south-east China, *c.*1690
Height: 13 cm

This round tea canister is decorated to a high standard with a sacred dragon, lizard and pheasants scampering among scudding clouds. It has a neat lid with a gated locking mechanism that served as a measure for the precious leaves – a feature emulated in the following century in the rococo version shown opposite.

FIG. 72
Chinese lacquer tray, *c.*1720
Length: 30 cm

In the eighteenth century Midlands businessmen such as John Baskerville were to make a fortune out of cheap and pretty japanned ware in imitation of this type of Chinese tray. At the same time, Liverpool and Worcester manufacturers were pioneering reproductions of blue-and-white Chinese porcelain, setting a trend that was to alter the face of industrial Britain and disrupt patterns of world trade as the popular passion for tea spread to all levels of society.

FIG. 74
Eighteenth-century teaware set up in the Walnut Room in Strangers' Hall, Norwich

This re-creation of an eighteenth-century tea setting shows the elegant equipage required for preparing the most fashionable of all Georgian beverages. The Lowestoft porcelain tea set – comprised of a teapot and stand, sugar bowl and cover, slop bowl, two plates, baluster-shaped tea canister and cover, tea bowl and saucer – is made of soft-paste porcelain. All the components are decorated in polychrome enamel colours and gilt, in a design known as the 'Jodrell' pattern, adapted from a Chinese motif. The silver sugar nips and mote spoon are *c.*1730–40. The purpose of the 'mote spoon' has been much debated, but it is probable that the pointed stem was intended to clear blocked tea leaves from the teapot spout, while the pierced bowl was used either to skim off floating leaves from the surface of the tea or to extract tea from the narrow-necked tea canisters of the period. The silver kettle is the earliest surviving example of an English tea-kettle and was made in London in 1694/5; its stand was made by John East in 1700/1. A similar example can be seen in *An English Family at Tea* by Joseph van Aken (fig. 75). On the floor is a silver and shagreen leather case by Samuel Taylor of London, containing two tea canisters and a sugar dish.

Thomas Tryon, a contemporary of William Salmon, referred to this predilection when dismissing coffee-drinking as a modish fad:

> *In a word, coffee is the drunkard's settle-brain, the fool's pastime, who admires it for being the production of Asia, and is ravished with delight when he hears the berries grow in the deserts of Asia, but would not give a farthing for an hogshead of it, if it were to be had on Hampstead-Heath or Banstead Downs.*[10]

A number of other exotic medicinal beverages were introduced into England at this time, among them china (*Smilax china* L.), a sarsaparilla-like drink from Cochin China, and salep, a mucilaginous and highly nutritious beverage obtained from the tubers of a number of eastern Mediterranean orchids (*Ophrys* spp.). Both were acquired tastes, enjoying a brief vogue but never catching on beyond the confines of the sickroom.

Despite its popularity at court and its reputation as a powerful medicament, tea took longer than chocolate and coffee to gain acceptance in England. By the 1730s, however, even though tea was the most expensive of the three new beverages, its consumption had started to overtake that of the other two. A growing taste for all things Chinese ensured that this costly luxury item came to the forefront of aristocratic fashion. Oriental porcelain had been highly valued since the end of the sixteenth century, but it only became readily available in Europe after the formation of the East India Company in the early 1600s. Before the introduction of tea, porcelain was used chiefly to dress out the expensive foods of the banquet or dessert course. The rise in popularity of quasi-oriental tea-drinking rituals created a lucrative market for the correct equipage and the demand for Chinese teawares soon began to outstrip supply, bringing considerable financial opportunities for British craftsmen. An exotic eastern element had suddenly been grafted on to an aristocratic lifestyle based on notions of classical culture. The drinking of a beverage which, a generation before, had been considered no more than an oriental curiosity had become a thoroughly modern and civilized activity.

Wealthy patrons by the dozen commissioned the greatest artists of the day to paint family portraits in which *à la mode* tea chests, tea bowls, silver kettles, urns, tea-tables and trays featured prominently as symbols of status and high fashion. Joseph van Aken's *An English Family at Tea* of *c.*1720 (fig. 75) is typical of these conversation pieces. Against a country house background of Ionic

FIG. 75
Joseph van Aken (*c.*1699–1749),
An English Family at Tea, *c.*1720
Oil on canvas, 99.4 × 116.2 cm

Teatime is here an aristocratic privilege, an attribute of a leisured and cultured existence. The colonnaded background vaguely suggests the spoils of the Grand Tour, but there is nothing vague about the depiction of the ceremony of taking tea and its accoutrements, expensive props that were displayed with pride. A lacquered table with its matching tray stands upon a Turkey carpet. At the hostess's foot sits the lacquered tea chest from which she has selected the chosen brew and is meticulously tipping into its lid the required amount. The maid stands poised to pour boiling water from the silver kettle into the tall redware pot (see fig. 70), which rests on a blue-and-white Chinese porcelain stand, part of the gold-rimmed service that also includes tall chocolate cups with handles. Notice also the stack of used tea bowls that stand in the slop bowl.

The handled cups await the jug of chocolate appearing from the right, the messy and energetic business of beating it to a froth having been performed off-stage in the kitchen. Unctuous and velvety in texture, the chocolate drink of this period was extremely rich in cocoa butter and was frequently fortified with wine or brandy.

columns and a statue of Bacchus, the hostess performs the ritual of measuring the precious leaf out of a canister from a lockable tea chest (see fig. 74). At this time, tea was subject to enormous excise duties, making it the most expensive of all household commodities. In 1728 we are told that 'the man at the Poultry has tea of all prices… Bohea from thirteen to twenty shillings, and green from twelve to thirty'.[11] It was no wonder that the maidservant could only be trusted to pour the water into the teapot. Other expensive goods, such as sugar, confectionery and spices, were also locked away in the closet by the mistress of the household to prevent pilfering by dishonest servants. It was through her role as custodian of the tea chest and its precious contents that the English gentlewoman came to preside over the making of tea.

Anne Wilson has noted another aspect of this interesting phenomenon:

> *The very costliness of the tea itself gave an extra cachet to the person who offered it at her entertainments – a psychological advantage which in due course helped to spread tea drinking further and further down the social scale.*[12]

Servants employed in large households were among the first working-class Englishmen and women to develop a taste for the drink, and a stipulation that they should receive two or three cups a day became a common feature of their terms of employment. Large towns saw the opening of dry tea and coffee shops, such as that opened in London's Strand in 1717 by Thomas Twining. City pleasure gardens also contributed to the spread of the habit (see fig. 78).

In the early years of the eighteenth century the prohibitive cost of tea meant that it was unobtainable by the less well-off, for whom William Salmon enthusiastically recommended a substitute made from dried sloe leaves: 'I commend our English sloe leaves in the place of the Indian Tea, since the Wisest of Mortals can't distinguish them when scalded.' Salmon's innocent suggestion led to a huge trade in counterfeit tea based on sloe and hawthorn leaves blended with a little authentic tea, a mixture that became known in the later eighteenth century as 'smouch'.[13]

Although tea became an important feature of breakfast for the gentry, taking the place of beer by the 1730s (see previous chapter), it was also drunk after dinner and at intervals throughout the day as a refreshment, accompanied by no more than a biscuit or a slice of toast, as in Zoffany's portrait of James Farrel Phipps (fig. 76). The earliest evidence of a more substantial meal based

FIG. 76
Johann Zoffany (1733?–1810),
James Farrel Phipps, *c.*1780
Oil on canvas, 76 × 61 cm

James Farrel Phipps graduated from Oxford at the time when James Boswell was endeavouring to establish himself as a smart young man about town. Both seem to have seen an elegant tea-table as part of a gentleman's necessary equipment. Boswell, constrained by a meagre allowance of £250 a year, had to strike a fine balance between outward show and private comforts. He budgeted £9 for tea and sugar, which he kept in a locked chest in his room. Young Phipps, who was from a wealthy West Indian family, seems to have attached the same importance to tea and is here seen cheerful and relaxed, taking a somewhat naïve pleasure in the reminder of his student nickname inscribed on the book in his hand: 'All Eggs / under the / Grate' (Alexander the Great). Boswell's intellectual aspirations may have been more elevated, but he would have envied Phipps his elegant tea equipage – a black lacquered tea board to protect the table, a set of European porcelain in the Chinese style, and a sugar bowl covered with a plate of what appears to be slices of teabread or Naples biscuit. That tea should have been the chosen tipple of an acknowledged young rake, who bred fighting cocks and was renowned for 'drowning the fatigues of war in a social bowl', is as significant as Boswell's omission of any kind of spirituous liquor from his annual budget.

Maturity caught up with them both, however, Phipps becoming MP for Peterborough and serving with Joseph Banks' first expedition to Newfoundland, and Boswell settling down to a life as a conscientious lawyer and immortal biographer.

Fig. 77
Marcellus Laroon (1679–1772)
A Musical Tea Party, 1740
Oil on canvas, 91.4 × 71.1 cm

This social gathering in a courtly setting, possibly the palace at Kew, reinforces the role of tea as the expensive baptismal liquid of the Georgian Age. The coarse merriment of other kinds of parties persisted alongside this, as Hogarth frequently reminds us, but Laroon excelled in his presentations of fashionable company enjoying smart food and drink in grand surroundings. Here the singers and other musicians are on the social level of the soberly clad servants who pass round tea and refreshments, while the ritual of preparing and serving the tea seems to have greater appeal than the music.

around tea is to be found in the Reverend Stotherd Abdy's journal of his visit to Berkshire in 1770, in which he makes numerous allusions to the meals of the day and the times at which they were served. We are informed that on Monday 10 September, while on a journey to Welford to visit the Houblon family, his party dined at the Pelican Inn in Newbury, at the old-fashioned hour of three o'clock, on veal cutlets and roasted rabbit. Within half an hour of arriving at the Houblon manse between six and seven, 'we had seated ourselves in the drawing room, Tea, and Coffee and many eatables of the Cake and Bread and Butter kind were brought.' This repast was followed at ten o'clock by a substantial supper of 'seven very elegant dishes'. From other entries in Abdy's journal it would appear that the Houblon family habitually consumed a light evening spread of bread, cakes, coffee and tea to break up the long seven-hour wait between dinner and supper.[14]

Here we see the origin of teatime in a light snack designed to alleviate the tedium of the long country house day. However, we need to examine more than the domestic life of the gentry in order to understand how another kind of tea meal evolved at the opposite end of the social scale. This meal developed in the 1780s as a result of drastic alterations to the diet of the labouring poor, precipitated by steep rises in the cost of beer resulting from serious grain shortages. In 1784 the high taxes on tea were reduced in response to the lobbying of Richard Twining, Chairman of the London Tea Dealers, which rendered the beverage an economical substitute for overpriced beer. By the end of the century much of the working-class population of southern England had became addicted to tea and grave concern was being voiced about the detrimental effect of this new habit on people's diet. The fears of the writer and political reformer William Cobbett as to the consequences of substituting tea, a drink with no nutritional value, for wholesome home-brewed ale are well known (see caption to fig. 78, p.119), but there were others who expressed equal anxiety. Perhaps the most vocal critic of the working man's newly acquired dependency on the brew was the physician William Buchan, who aired his views in his pamphlet *Observations concerning the Diet of the Common People* (1797).

Buchan's thoughts on tea tell us just how entrenched it had become in the everyday life of the English cottager and his family by the closing years of the eighteenth century. He informs us that:

> *... the greatest consumption of bread is occasioned by tea. It is said that the subjects of Great Britain consume a greater quantity of*

FIG. 78
George Morland (1763–1804),
The Tea Garden, *c*.1790
Oil on canvas, 40.6 × 50.5 cm

This sentimental painting of a family enjoying an outing to one of London's pleasure gardens marks the exact point in the trickle-down of tea from an expensive aristocratic beverage to a cheap popular brew. No longer an exclusive habit, it was on its way to becoming the British national drink. William Cobbett, several decades later, was to fulminate against the harm that 'this vile concoction' was doing to the morale and health of the labouring classes. In his *Cottage Economy* he expounds the nutritional virtues of beer compared with 'the corrosive, gnawing, and poisonous powers of tea', stating that tea drives lads to the public house (where the beer is inferior to home-brew) and does little less for the girls, to whom 'the gossip of the tea-table is no bad preparatory school for the brothel'.[15]

The innocent group depicted here seem quite unaware of the perilous downward slope they are on as they indulge in a harmless leisure activity in which the whole family can participate. Grand-parents, proud father, mother in an outrageous pink bonnet, baby, dog and lively boy and girl all happily partake of the 'corrosive, gnawing, and poisonous' brew. This semi-rural setting is a long way from the elegant drawing rooms of London society. The plain wooden table has a cheap laquered tray of inexpensive blue-and-white transfer crockery and the waiter in the background hurries along with a stoneware teapot characteristic of the Midlands potteries that flourished as middle-class families emulated the genteel habits of their betters.

> *that herb, than the whole inhabitants of all the nations of this quarter of the globe. The lowest woman in England must have her tea, and the children generally share it with her. As tea contains no nourishment, either for young or old, there must of course be bread and butter to eat along with it. The quartern loaf will not go far among a family of hungry children, and if we add the cost of tea, sugar, butter, and milk, the expense of one meal will be more than would be sufficient to fill their bellies with wholesome food.*[16]

He was particularly concerned about the risks to health caused by the high consumption of butter at tea meals of this kind.

> *I have been astonished to see the quantities of butter eaten by gross women who lead sedentary lives. Their tea-bread is generally contrived so as to suck up butter like a spunge. What quantities of crumpets and muffins they will devour in a morning, soaked with this oil; and afterwards complain of indigestion, when they have eaten what would overload the stomach of a ploughman.*[17]

Buchan's answer to these problems was to persuade the poor to abandon expensive tea-drinking and return to a wholesome regimen of vegetable pottage and boiled grains, a diet that would have been familiar to the Hertford-shire harvesters of an earlier generation, as described by William Ellis (see p.73). However, he found that some addicts were beyond redemption:

> *There is reason to believe that one half the bread consumed in England is used to tea, without one hearty meal ever being made of it. The higher ranks use tea as a luxury, while the lower orders make a diet of it. I had lately occasion to see a striking instance of this in a family that was represented to me as in distress for want of bread. I sent them a little money, and was informed that they ran with it to the tea-shop.*[18]

From Buchan's observations it is clear that, for the poor of southern England, tea had become a meal in its own right, and for many the only meal. There is a world of difference between this working-class version of tea and the polite early evening repast consumed at Welford as a stopgap between a heavy three o'clock dinner and an elegant ten o'clock supper. In the lean and desolate opening decades of the nineteenth century, the diet of the poor became even worse. Anne Wilson has described the plight of the south country labourer at this time:

> *Tea was a necessity for such people. High food prices, enclosure and their general poverty had reduced them to a monotonous diet of bread, cheese and occasionally bacon. Through lack of fuel they had lost the art of making warm soups and pottages, and indeed had lost the taste for them too. Tea was not simply their sole liquid to wash down their dry meals; it was also the only warm and comforting element in their diet.*[19]

Even when times got better, bread and other baked goods, washed down with plenty of tea, remained at the heart of the meal shared by the family when the menfolk returned from the fields or the mill. This was to become the family tea of the Victorian age. Improvements in kitchen technology, such as the hot-air oven, enabled many poorer families to make their own home-baked bread and cakes. When they could afford them, luxuries such as potted meats, raised pies and ham were added to make the teatime spread even more appealing, especially on high days and holidays. The term 'high tea' seems to have emerged in the 1840s to describe this more luxurious form of tea, which included meat. It probably evolved out of a desire to develop a more formal dinner-like spread from the common tea meal of the working family and appears to have become popular first in Scotland and northern England. The growing influence of the temperance movement also encouraged the pious working-class family to adopt tea as the main beverage drunk at the meal. Laura Mason has argued that the buffet-like high tea is a fossilized form of the seventeenth- and eighteenth-century dinner, with sweets mixed among the savouries and a wide range of dishes from which to make your individual choices.[20]

By the late nineteenth century high tea had become sufficiently respectable to enter the standard middle-class repertoire of meals. An 1892 edition of Isabella Beeton's *Book of Household Management* informs us:

> *In some houses it is a permanent institution, quite taking the place of late dinner, and to many it is a most enjoyable meal, young people preferring it to dinner, it being a movable feast that*

FIG. 79
Sir Hubert von Herkomer (1849–1914),
Eventide: A Scene in Westminster Union, 1878
Oil on canvas, 110.5 × 198.5 cm

Herkomer (the Sir and the *von* came later with success and prosperity) was of humble origin, and much of his early work as an illustrator for the *Graphic* magazine showed a concern for the poor and underprivileged. The woodcut on which this painting is based is altogether more bleak in content and execution. It does not include the friendly tea-tray and the homely cups and saucers, and here the touches of sweetness, a posy of flowers and a wholesome young lady cutting out fabric for the obligatory 'work', add warmth and colour to what was originally a starkly uncomfortable scene. 'Truth in art should be enhanced by sentiment,' Herkomer felt, and here, in a rare but popular painting of this troubling subject matter, he gave his clients not only the truth but also the reassurance they must have needed. The toothless gums suck gratefully at the tea, but the fingers, gnarled by arthritis, must still stitch on – for these are the deserving poor, glad to receive the care that the profligate and feckless needy cannot claim, but still constrained to toil for their keep, such as it is. Indeed, the diet in prisons and workhouses at the time was deliberately meagre, on the principle that anything which gave the poor the energy to get above themselves would be a misuse of charity. The tea, bread and jam and gruel might have been mitigated by antiscorbutic potatoes or green vegetables, but the next decade would bring further nutritional deterioration, when mechanically rolled white flour eliminated essential nutrients from the bread. These old ladies were the frail survivors of decades of poor diet. They had escaped an infant mortality of

43 per cent in children under twelve in the first decade of the century, progressing from an adolescence subject to rickets to an adulthood threatened by tuberculosis, anæmia and all the ailments associated with poor housing and inadequate nutrition.

can be partaken of at hours which will not interfere with tennis, boating or other amusements, and but little formality is needed.[21]

This adoption by the Victorian 'respectable' classes of a meal that started life as a spread for the working family is unique in the history of English gastronomy – the tendency has always been for food traditions to percolate down rather than up the social scale.

FIG. 80
Henry Herbert La Thangue (1859–1929),
The Connoisseur: a portrait of Abraham Mitchell, 1887
Oil on canvas, 114 × 160 cm

When the successful Bradford mill-owner Abraham Mitchell moved out of the crowded, industrial city that his entrepreneurial energies had helped create, he chose sixty acres of secluded parkland on the hills above Bradford and built himself a house, Bowling Park, with his own private art gallery. His enlightened patronage of the arts and active role in the political life of his native city made him and his fellow captains of industry feel superior, morally if not socially, to the old landed aristocracy remote from the social problems of the time. Rural unrest seemed to many more unsettling than the brash, raw energies of a frontier town such as Bradford, which trebled its population between 1831 and 1851 and was rapidly taking the lead over Halifax in the worsted industry of West Yorkshire. Patronage of the arts and active involvement in improving the quality of life in the city was a feel-good factor in the lives of these rich and benevolent magnates. Painters like Henry La Thangue, himself from Huguenot Yorkshire stock, had a strong commitment to recording the lives of the rural poor, and his moral force and modern methods appealed to these tough, hard-nosed Bradford folk who felt that their own modern down-to-earth business methods would be the salvation of the country. La Thangue painted this group portrait of the Mitchell family in 1887. The scene, though informal, indicates the importance of the gallery in the life of the family – tea is ready, but the others wait deferentially while the head of the household scrutinizes his latest acquisition with a magnifying glass with the same intensity that he focuses on his worsted production. The table setting consists of flowers in an aesthetic vase, a teapot and some tiny cups. This is in contrast to the traditional Yorkshire tea that sustained workers between shifts down the mill. Or the lavish spreads that tempted Charlotte Brontë's despised race of curates to flock uninvited to cottage homes on baking day, when teacakes, parkin, jam tarts, curd cake and plates full of bread and butter provided the calories that kept out the all-pervasive cold and damp in unheated homes and workplaces.

Despite these new developments, the upper-class afternoon tea remained more or less unaltered. It had become the polite 'At Home' described in late nineteenth-century editions of Beeton, a meal that would have been recognizable to the gentry of the previous century as the light collation between afternoon dinner and late supper:

> *At the regular At Home, one held on a certain day every week or month, to which only one invitation is given, by card or on a visiting one, nothing more is expected than some tea, thin bread-and-butter and cakes.*

To add to the confusion, there was another tea meal, also described as an 'At Home', which was more complex:

> *Here we have, in addition to the above, such things as ices, claret and champagne cup (if in season), sandwiches, small fancy ones as a rule, such as foie gras or cucumber, a great variety of small sweets, and, in fact, just the same kind of light refreshments usually served at a dance.*[22]

As we enter the twenty-first century the British passion for drinking tea has not abated, but the traditional meals associated with the beverage are becoming rarer and are no longer served in many homes. Perhaps both high tea and afternoon tea will eventually become as obsolete as the social rituals and niceties of the Victorian 'At Home'.

Fig. 81
Vanessa Bell (1879–1961),
Nursery Tea, 1911
Oil on canvas, 76.9 × 105.3 cm

This scene almost certainly depicts Vanessa Bell's own children. Vanessa's sister, Virginia Woolf, seemed to enjoy the rough-and-tumble of her expeditions to the Register Office to procure servants for Vanessa, who had problems finding nursemaids for her two sons and baby daughter. The ensuing clashes of personality, as Virginia organized swaps between the two households, would have tried the patience of more saintly serving girls than Nellie Britain and Nelly Boxall, seen here in uncharacteristically solemn mood, supervising in starched white aprons a sedate nursery tea. This bears no resemblance to the merry family gatherings in Vanessa's photograph albums, where unruly naked infants pee into teacups and play pagan games in the garden. The very plain tea of bread, butter and milk is characteristic of the wholesome fare also enjoyed by house guests (exhorted in wartime to bring their own butter), who sat down to roast beef and apple pie in a pleasant holiday environment where the unconventional behaviour of the adults contrasted with the structured security of the life of these much-loved children.

Fig. 82: Aerial view (left)
Fig. 83: General view
Nursery tea, *c.*1934, re-created in the nursery at Stranger's Hall, Norwich

This rosy picture evokes the kind of tea setting enjoyed by the children of the comfortably-off, tucked safely away from the outside world in the sanctuary of the nursery. The Bunnykins tableware designs have an enduring appeal and remain popular today. The first designs were by Sister Barbara Vernon Bailey, daughter of Cuthbert Bailey, who became Royal Doulton's General Manager in 1925. Vernon's watercolours were launched on a new nurseryware range in 1934. Although the war interrupted production and some shapes were not continued in peacetime, the factory went on to make numerous variations on the rabbit's humorous antics, using the talents of other members of Doulton's staff after Sister Barbara decided to devote more time to her religious life.

Watching the proceedings from their lofty perch on the chest of drawers are three 'Bunnykins Old Figures' introduced in 1939 and withdrawn during World War II. From left to right stand Farmer Bunnykins, Mother Bunnykins and (with one ear cocked) Mary Bunnykins. Acting as a master of ceremonies down on the table itself is Reggie Bunnykins. Accompanying the rabbit entourage on the chest is a Bunny-shaped teapot (introduced in 1939), an extremely rare example, whose beady eye must have kept any errant infant in check.[23]

The food is simple, easily digestible stuff arranged on a Doulton tablecloth of the period. Boiled eggs and bread and butter are followed by delicate slices of Madeira cake or a shortbread biscuit or two. This setting shows that the quintessentially British tradition of teatime was not just the preserve of the grown-ups.

FIG. 84
Andreas Duncan Carse (1876–1938),
The Mannequins, *c.*1930
Oil on canvas, 63.5 × 91.5 cm

In Bournemouth a faint glimpse of the *douceur de vivre* of seaside life before the First World War comes to the visitor lingering on what was once the remote cliff path where Merton and Annie Russell-Cotes built a gracious home to house their eccentric, enthusiastic, eclectic collection of treasures and works of art. Things had already changed almost beyond recognition by the eve of World War II, when the widow of Andreas Duncan Carse presented this painting of a typical seaside hotel tea-room to the Museum and Gallery which the Russell-Cotes had bequeathed to the town. Carse was a versatile artist, readily turning his hand from murals for the *Queen Mary* to lively children's book illustrations and genre scenes. *The Mannequins* typifies the social changes that were creeping along the south coast in a tide of bricks and concrete, as remote from the exclusive private collector's eyrie as are today's brash hotels, office blocks and conference centres. The clients are from all walks of life, and the genteel provincial atmosphere is a long way from the glitter of the metropolis. The decor is 'modern' but not outrageous, with tactful concealed lighting and functional furniture. The flimsy light-coloured frocks of the mannequins contrast with the conventional but rather dull styles worn by the other women present. The party at the table on the left use clichéd gestures of a studied elegance that ape, but alas cannot match, the style to which they aspire. On the right a modest, rather dowdy family, undistracted by the fashion show, settles down to the usual fare of bread and butter, muffins in a covered dish, eclairs and sponge cake with cream filling and meringues, served from what seems to be a functional catering service rather than the silver and porcelain of more chic establishments.

A. Duncan Carse

CHAPTER **5**

The Great Outdoors

OUTDOOR eating has a long history in Britain. Posidonius (135–52 BC) wrote about Celtic meals where the men sat on the ground on straw or hides and ate meat with their fingers

> *in a cleanly but leonine fashion, raising up whole limbs in both hands and biting off the meat, while any part that is hard to tear off they cut through with a small dagger… Beside them are hearths blazing with fire, with cauldrons and spits containing large pieces of meat. Brave warriors they honour with the finest portions of the meat.*[1]

Teenage sons and daughters waited on them; other women ate elsewhere. Posidonius's Celts lived in Gaul, but their cousins in Britain would have eaten in identical fashion.

In medieval times, too, feasts for large numbers of people were held in the open air if the indoor space of the great hall was inadequate, and during far-ranging expeditions it was clearly necessary to eat outdoors. An illustration in Turberville's *Book of Faulconrie* of 1575 (fig. 86) shows Queen Elizabeth enjoying a hunt picnic of cold fowls and wine. However, in his text Turberville suggests that the 'chief personage' at the hunt should watch the breaking up of the deer and eat 'carbonadies' (grilled steaks) cut straight from the kill, along with a fine sauce based on wine and spices and newly prepared over a chafing dish. Meanwhile he or she would summon those who had performed best during the hunt and 'reward them favourably as hath been the custom of all noble personages to do'.[2] Thus brave huntsmen were now receiving the finest meat, once the prerogative of brave Celtic warriors.

The outdoor meal on home territory was also popular. By late medieval times the gardens of yeomen farmers and manorial families often contained a purpose-built arbour, framed with vines or honeysuckle to create a shaded area. Here, in hot weather, food and drink were brought out and set on a trestle table.

Fig. 85

Thomas Rowlandson (1756–1827), *Richmond Bridge*, *c.*1808–15 (detail)
Watercolour on paper, 27.9 × 42.6 cm

It is difficult to see what food this animated group of picknickers are eating, but they have already consumed at least three bottles of wine, with another five yet to go.

A fresco of about 1600 (fig. 36), illustrating the parable of the Return of the Prodigal Son, shows that inns, too, provided customers with a pleasant shady arbour in which to partake of a summer meal. A realistic detail is the landlady adding up the bill on her slate. It is evident from the female guests present why respectable women did not frequent inns on their own at that period.

Country house life burgeoned for the aristocracy and gentry during the sixteenth century. Families entertained and visited each other in their fine new or recently improved houses. A novel addition to their dinners was the 'banquet' or dessert course, served in a separate place from the main meal. In summer this might be an arbour, or a banqueting house sited to offer attractive views across the garden and beyond – on an artificial mound, coupled at either end of a raised terrace, in a tower, or even on the roof of the house (see opposite page). After consuming their sweetmeats the guests would move outside to converse with friends while admiring the view of the bowling green or formal garden.[3]

The banquet provided an opportunity for conspicuous consumption all through the seventeenth century, when only the well-to-do could afford to be lavish with sugar. Others contented themselves with gingerbread and spiced or fruited buns sold at fairs and markets and cried through town streets. Outdoor workers spent short mealbreaks close to their workplaces, and by 1600 they could expect both a mid-morning and a mid-afternoon break, preceded by one for breakfast if they had made an early start. The two later breaks were often called either 'nuncheon' (a traditional word going back to the *non shench*, noontime drink, of Anglo-Saxon times) or 'bever' (from Old French *beivre*, to drink). Both words were still current at the end of Queen Victoria's reign.[4]

For agricultural labourers the basic fare was ale or beer with bread; cheese or cold bacon was added if available. Confusingly, the lump of cheese was sometimes called a

'luncheon' of cheese and the slice of bacon a 'lunch' for some two hundred years before those words were applied, around 1800, to the newly invented meal we eat today.[5] The farmworker consumed his nuncheon or bever under a tree or hedge. At harvest-time the farmer's wife contributed apple pies, pasties or other extras. William Ellis described in 1750 how seedcakes, made for the purpose, were carried out to harvesters in Hertfordshire as 'beaver victuals... about four o'clock in the afternoon with some cheese, for the Harvest-men to eat this cake dry with or to dip it in ale.'[6] In East Yorkshire such food, called 'lowance', might include currant pasties, hamcake (also a kind of pasty) and hot 'sadcake' (a lard cake) running with butter.[7] The harvestmen laboured for long hours to take full advantage of daylight, but the event did give some variety to their diet.

In towns, outdoor workers such as builders, porters and rivermen had year-round variety if they chose to make up their meals from food sold by hawkers in the streets. There were oysters (cheap until they became scarce in the later nineteenth century), boiled whelks and mussels, pickled herrings, sheep's trotters, black puddings and other inexpensive cooked meats, fruit, gingerbread, buttermilk and whey. Cookshops supplied pies and pasties to take away. Court records offer glimpses of London's street traders. One from January 1710 mentions people 'with wheelbarrows wherein they carry oysters, oranges, decayed cheese, apples, nuts, gingerbread and other wares to sell'. Another, more or less contemporary, tells of a woman whose business had been 'selling fruit and oysters, crying hot-pudding and gray-peas in the street, and like'.[8]

Townspeople of the middling sort enjoyed outdoor meals in the seventeenth and eighteenth centuries informally at home, in larger gardens elsewhere, or on river trips. Samuel Pepys and his neighbour Sir William Penn went out onto the 'leads' (flat roofs) of their houses on the hot evening of 5 June 1665 'and there we stayed talking and singing and drinking of great draughts of claret and eating botargo and bread and butter till 12 at night, it being moonshine'.

The earliest pleasure garden, Spring Garden at Vauxhall, was opened to the public in 1661. It was laid out with paths enclosing areas of 'wilderness', and its nightingales were famous. Food and drink were sold there, but they were expensive and thrifty visitors brought their own. Londoners also walked in nursery gardens, such as the Neat House gardens, near Chelsea, and later Brompton Park. Here the proprietors sold wine and beer, but visitors took their own food.[9] Pepys and his companions went 'by coach to the Neathouses' on 1 August 1667, and 'there in a box in a tree we sat and sang and talked and eat'.

FIG. 86
Detail from an anonymous woodcut illustrated in the *Book of Faulconrie* (London 1575) by George Turberville (*c.*1540–*c.*1610), showing Elizabeth I (1533–1603) at a hunt picnic

FIG. 87
Johann Zoffany (1733?–1810), *The Dashwood and Auriol Families*, 1783–7
Oil on canvas, 158 × 216 cm

Johann Zoffany sailed to India in 1783, appearing on the ship's books as midshipman while laying claim to the title Sir John. He returned in 1790, temporarily shattered by the experience of shipwreck and cannibalism but having enjoyed years of lucrative commissions and agreeable socializing with the fashionable English society in Lucknow and Calcutta. His prickly ambition and charismatic energies had fitted well into the slightly raffish, brittle lifestyle associated with the East India Company. Whilst his many family group portraits portray the decorum of English manners and fashions, Zoffany also painted huge canvases celebrating the splendours of life in India, such as hunting parties with magnificently bedecked nabobs and their retinues. His group portrait of the Dashwood and Auriol families (which took four years to complete) tingles with some of this excitement – the two families take tea under a shady tree, with native servants performing the polite and very English ritual for them in an exotic setting whose backdrop affords glimpses of Calcutta and the vast landscape beyond. The fine silver teapot is typical of the cylindrical examples being produced at the time, attended by a pair of fashionable vase-shaped containers for tea and sugar. But the scene is far from static. There is movement and a hint of events unfolding in a wider context. At either side of the canvas messengers have arrived and Captain Charles Auriol on the left and his brother James on the right must prepare to depart for intrepid adventures.

The Vauxhall garden, remodelled by Jonathan Tyers and reopened in 1732 (admission charge a shilling a head) became more popular than ever. Visitors thronged the wide avenues, listened to outdoor concerts and consumed tea, wine and light meals served in the 'arbours', a series of alcoves backed by trees and facing onto the North and South walks.[10] Fashionable ladies took tea there, and so too, on their days off, did their maidservants, clad in their mistresses' cast-off gowns and enjoying their opportunity to be fashionable themselves. The pleasure gardens around London and the larger provincial towns helped spread the tea-drinking habit from aristocratic circles through the rest of society.[11]

At Ranelagh the one shilling entrance fee included a 'regale' of tea or coffee and bread and butter. A sarcastic commentator wrote in the *London Magazine* in 1774 that visitors 'stare about them for half an hour, laugh at other fools who are drenching and scalding themselves with coffee and tea ... and then they trail home again to sup.'[12] At Vauxhall a more substantial meal could be purchased in the gardens, but some visitors brought food in from outside. According to Horace Walpole, in June 1750 Lady Caroline Petersham and her friends 'minced seven chickens into a china dish and stewed them over a lamp with three pats of butter and a flagon of water' at Vauxhall. She also 'brought Betty the fruit-girl with hampers of strawberries and cherries from Rogers's, and made her wait upon us, and then made her sup by us at a little table'.[13]

Another favourite venue for outdoor eating was a boat, or a riverbank reached by boat. When Pepys travelled by barge to visit naval ships moored on a lower reach of the Thames, he and his companions took along 'some bottles of wine and beer and neats' tongues' and passed the time on board singing, drinking and eating, and were 'exceeding merry.'[14] On evening trips upriver, he and his wife occasionally consumed wine and cold meat on the boat. At Barn Elms they disembarked and strolled about, and there on 26 May 1667 'with great pleasure we saw some gallant ladies and people come with their bottles and baskets and chairs and forms to sup under the trees by the waterside'. The folk in Rowlandson's watercolour (fig. 85), sharing a meal on the riverbank near Richmond Bridge around 1800, are less elegant to behold than Pepys' 'gallant ladies', but they are enjoying themselves just as much.

About this time two very different developments began to redefine the outdoor meal. The romantic movement, with its stress on awe-inspiring scenery and picturesque ruins, encouraged people to visit distant viewpoints, often by carriage but making the final approach on foot. If the party was at all large, several servants and even an extra carriage were needed to carry the provisions.

The second defining influence on the meal taken along on an excursion was the emergence of its distinctive name. The word picnic (borrowed from French *pique-nique*) originally indicated an indoor shared meal to which each person contributed a dish from a pre-arranged menu. In 1802 a group of young society people in London founded the Picnic Club, where they shared meals sent in from a tavern and followed them up with amateur theatricals and concerts. Because they were often in the news, 'picnic' became a well-known term, and soon it began to signify an outdoor meal based on contributions from two or three families who joined forces to visit a distant beauty spot or viewpoint.[15]

The other newly-coined meal name of the time was luncheon, and at first luncheon resembled a picnic in that it comprised food carried by the eater to a venue away from home. This is what Dorothy Wordsworth meant when she wrote in her journal for 4 May 1802, about a break during a day's walking near Keswick: 'William and I ate a luncheon, then went on towards the waterfall.' Sometimes the solid food for a luncheon was taken to an inn, where the innkeeper supplied wine or beer to complete the meal.[16] That custom continued in country areas until the coming of the freezer and the microwave oven, with the picnickers usually sitting at the pub's outdoor tables to eat their meal.

Very suitable for a simple meal was the sandwich, invented in about 1760 by the eponymous 4th Earl, who found it convenient when spending long hours at the gaming table.[17] But it is practical outdoor food too, in the absence of cutlery, since the greasy elements are all on the inside and fingers make contact only with the dry outer surface of the bread.

Pies were also convenient. We remember the pigeon pies for the picnic on Box Hill in Jane Austen's *Emma*; gooseberry pies in other nineteenth-century picnic menus; and of course Sam Weller's 'weal pie' at the shooting picnic in Dickens' *Pickwick Papers*.[18] Various cold roast meats, ham, tongue, cheese, fruit and bread and butter were also common picnic foods. By mid-Victorian times these might be augmented by cold salmon and lobster, salads, stewed fruit packed in well-corked jars, cheesecakes, biscuits and several cold puddings – cold plum pudding being a particular favourite. The accompanying beverages were cold and alcoholic: wine, beer, champagne, brandy and rum are those most often mentioned.

The tea-picnic developed after the emergence of tea as a small meal taken some three hours after the middle-day meal.[19] Tea in the garden became a special summer pleasure, and Victorian families liked to be photographed there, clustered around the tea-table. Artists painted variations on the theme,

FIG. 88
William Holman Hunt (1827–1910),
The Children's Holiday, 1864–5
Oil on canvas, 214 × 147 cm

In September of 1864 William Holman Hunt, only recently disentangled, at some expense, from the blandishments of the vivacious artist's model Annie Miller, was in no mood to enjoy the bland decorum of a respectable bourgeois household. The commission to paint Lady Fairbairn and five of her seven children was dutifully executed, if somewhat resentfully: 'I have not the love of the country general among artists, not enough to make me quite happy in it after the first two weeks of rusticating – however I shall have to stay another two, or, perhaps, three weeks.' A group portrait presented as an outdoor tea party was not a new concept, but in spite of his boredom Holman Hunt brings a freshness and sparkle to this family gathering, focused firmly on the figure of the mother, whose pride in her children is reinforced by the graceful use of symbols of fecundity. The ripe summer fruit, which the babe in the foreground balances on her plump little knees, matches the necklace of rosehips, themselves an echo of the pagan coral jewellery worn by her mother, while older siblings in the distance offer fruit to the tame deer in the middle distance. The food in this celebration of triumphant motherhood seems to be a token plate of buns, but the tea things and furnishings are a conscious display of affluence and Lady Fairbairn a willing clothes-horse for the fashionable striped silk dress and Paisley shawl. Hunt has strayed into the realm of still life with his accurate depiction of the tea-table, and he probably illustrates treasured heirlooms from the family collection. It is an assembly that spans several generations. The hot water urn, for example, was almost certainly made by the innovative silversmiths Francis Butty and Nicholas Dume around 1760. These urns were particularly useful for outdoor picnics some distance from the kitchen, and since they required no spirit lamps their efficacy was not subject to the vagaries of the summer breeze. The body, with a capacity of around six pints of hot water, unscrews from a rectangular base designed to support a heated iron plug. When reassembled and carried to the table by a rather nervous servant (they had a reputation for instability), they kept the water hot for a considerable time. The gilded lustre tea set seems to be of a later date. In Greek revival style, it bears similarities with designs 88 and 90 in Minton's pattern book No. 1 (started in 1800). The inverted pear-shaped silver teapot could date from the same period, although earlier examples with this exuberant chased decoration are well known.

such as William Holman Hunt's *The Children's Holiday* (fig. 88), in which the mother-figure presides over the tea urn.

The picnickers in Tissot's *Holyday* of *c.*1876 (fig. 89) have taken with them a spirit lamp to heat the tea-kettle and a tablecloth to define the meal area. With Sir James Guthrie's *Midsummer* (fig. 90) the garden-tea theme continues in deep shade, while Sir John Lavery's *The Table, St Fagan's Castle* (fig. 91) shows another family group assembled for tea out of doors.

Community celebrations often took the form of an open-air tea, laid out on trestle tables. Typical was the annual Sunday School feast: Charlotte Brontë describes one in *Shirley*, with tea and abundant currant buns for the children, and home-brewed ale and buns for their seniors.[20]

Fairs and markets also encouraged outdoor eating. A stall at Clifton Feast, depicted by Mary Ellen Best in 1835, would have sold moulded gingerbreads and gingerbread alphabets (to help children learn to spell) as well as cakes and sweets. Muffins, Banbury cakes, sweet China oranges and oysters were among the eatables cried in the streets of York in the 1820s.[21]

By mid-century there was a huge network of traders in London's streets, selling cakes, gingerbread, fruit, oysters, boiled whelks, sheep's trotters, pickled salmon, ginger beer. Others purveyed baked potatoes and fried fish costing 1d, with a slice of bread (chips were added from about 1870), hot eels and pea soup. The minimum equipment required to produce the last two was a fish-kettle, a soup-kettle, five basins, five cups, ten spoons, a washing-up basin, a board and trestle, and two tin saucepans 'in which charcoal is always burning to keep the eels and soup hot', according to Henry Mayhew.[22] Consumers included low-paid workers, and residents in poorer districts who came out to enjoy a tasty snack and a change from their monotonous home diet.

Meanwhile the better-off were developing the cult of the picnic. The preferred site, initially, was a grassy area in scenic countryside.[23] When the new railways made day trips to seaside resorts possible, the idea of the beach picnic emerged; road transport was still necessary to reach remote bays. Francis Kilvert, staying with friends at Ilston in Gower, South Wales, on 16 October 1878 'drove in the waggonette, and went down to Langland Bay, where we had luncheon among the rocks, the ladies drinking wine out of shells as the cups had been forgotten'.[24]

Customized picnic baskets were available by the 1880s. Major Landon designed his own, including a 'hunting luncheon-case' with a central division, one side for the meat pie or cold cutlets, the other for bread, cake or plum

FIG. 89
James Tissot (1836–1902), *Holyday (The Picnic)*, c.1876
Oil on canvas, 76.2 × 99.4 cm

James (originally Jacques Joseph) Tissot enjoyed both professional success and domestic happiness during his years in England. The backdrop for this painting of a picnic tea party is the garden of his own home in St John's Wood, London. We are seduced by the beauty of the setting, the autumn foliage and the elegant dress, of his skittish but essentially well-behaved young people, barely out of the nursery themselves and still quite content to enjoy a nursery tea chaperoned by the elderly couple on the left. Here there are no raffish antics or extravagant provisions, none of the overt salaciousness of other portrayals of meals out of doors – such as the louche young men about town and naked young women of doubtful repute in *Le Déjeuner sur l'Herbe* that so shocked and delighted Manet's contemporaries. Tissot endows that irrational English propensity to defy the elements and eat inappropriate things in conditions of considerable discomfort in the open air with the respectability conferred by Mrs Beeton: 'A well-arranged picnic is one of the pleasantest forms of entertainment.' The provisions here are bland and blameless: milky tea, soda water, a rather plain fruit cake and some thin bread and butter. An abundance of furs, rugs and cosy shawls provide protection from the late autumn chill; the old lady is well wrapped up and the young lads wear mufflers and jaunty caps denoting membership of 'I Zingari', a fashionable cricket club. To Oscar Wilde they were 'over-dressed, common-looking people', but to Tissot's public they were reassuringly free of the taint of 'Frenchness' and its associated impropriety.[25]

However, the setting contains just a hint of ambivalence, a sense that the suburban garden could in fact be the scene of equivocal relationships and departures from conventional morality, and a closer look at the body language of the various couples reveals complexities beyond the schoolroom innocence of our first impression.

Fig. 90
Sir James Guthrie (1859–1902), *Midsummer*, 1892
Oil on canvas, 101.8 × 126.6 cm

Guthrie applied fresh modern techniques to his depictions of the placid life of conventional middle-class ladies around Helensburgh on the Firth of Clyde, but the elements of this calm tea party in the shade were unlikely to have been as innovative as painting out of doors with a big flat brush must have seemed to his contemporaries. The traditional Scottish teatime fare of drop scones, Selkirk bannocks, Aberdeen butteries, Caledonian cream, honey cakes and petticoat tails might well have included the version of shortbread recorded in an early nineteenth-century cookery manuscript compiled by Margaret Stewart of Erskine, which was made more appealing than the familiar commercial version by including caraway seeds, almonds and candied orange peel.[26]

Fig. 91
Sir John Lavery (1856–1941), *The Table, St Fagan's Castle*, 1905
Oil on canvas, 55.8 × 116.8 cm

'The heat at St Fagan's was great and enchanting,' wrote Lady Paget in her diary. 'We had all our meals out of doors.' Seen here taking tea on the terrace, enjoying the view over the landscaped watergardens and woods beyond, is Lady Paget with her daughter and son-in-law Baron Windsor, Earl of Plymouth, together with their four

children. A brief escape from the castle's comfortable but somewhat gloomy Tudor dining room, with perhaps the hugest, darkest carved oak sideboard in Wales, must have been a relief on fine summer days, when even the new dining room, resplendent with the ornate furnishings deemed necessary for the dinners Baron Windsor gave in his role as Lord Mayor of Cardiff, must have seemed less agreeable than this small, pleasantly secluded terrace. The intimacy of the scene is characteristic of the family's easy relationship with the estate and the local people, for their frequent visits to St Fagan's and their concern for both the castle itself and the well-being of their tenants made the decades before and after this painting some of the happiest of its long history, culminating in the establishment in its grounds of the Welsh Folk Museum.

But the tea-table is unlikely to have had typical Welsh food on it, for the family employed an Italian chef and kitchen staff, and even the celebratory tea for the popular young Baron's coming-of-age in 1878 had been of the basic British kind. When fifty volunteer ladies served it up in a specially erected marquee to 3,182 local women and children (whose menfolk had enjoyed a fine roast lunch only a few hours before), 1,060 lbs of plum cake, 1,320 penny buns, 400 lbs of bread, 60 lbs of butter, 25 lbs of tea, 250 lbs of sugar and 25 gallons of milk were consumed.

Tea on the ducal terrace must have been agreeable, too, for the ambitious young John Lavery, then at the beginning of a glittering career, who had already come a long way from the Belfast orphanage and Glasgow apprenticeship of his early years. He seemed to be making the right impression on Lady Paget, whose diary records: 'At St Fagan's I did a good deal of sitting for various pictures. First to a naïve little Scotsman, Mr R. who adores Sargent, and then Mr Lavery, who has got a reputation, is Irish, and adores Whistler. Windsor had this picture painted as a record of himself, his wife and the children. It is a group on a garden terrace... Windsor is charmed with it.'

FIG. 92
Gerard Chowne (1875–1915),
After Lunch, 1910
Oil on canvas, 101.5 × 128 cm

William Rothenstein had a gift for friendship and a talent for reminiscence, and the summers he spent in France with his brother Albert and friends such as Gerard Chowne and his wife are summed up in this work, which Chowne probably painted at Vaucobles in Provence. The expatriate tendency to eat out of doors, against all common sense and prudence (while the locals were lunching in cool, dark dining rooms with the shutters tightly closed), must explain this lunch party on a terrace, whose participants are enjoying the luminous light and the view towards the distant sea. The oranges and cherries seem to indicate that it is spring, and the relaxed pose of the group, casually smoking at the end of a light lunch, holds all the promise of a long idyllic summer, unclouded by any intimation of the war to come – in which the artist would perish.

pudding. Whisky or brandy and aerated water were carried separately in flasks. Another more elaborate basket had space inside for two pint bottles, 'one for champagne or claret, the other for sherry or Salutaris water', and was fitted up with four horn cups, pepper, salt and mustard, cutlery and plates for two people, 'and a portable table is fastened outside.'[27]

The Edwardians had tea-baskets fitted with a spirit stove, a combined teapot and kettle, crockery, cutlery and labelled tins for biscuits, cakes, bread and butter, salt, etc. They could also purchase special sets of greaseproof paper plates and dishes sold for picnics in several sizes.[28] The 'Thermos' vacuum flask was invented in 1907. Florence Jack wrote in 1911: 'Wealthy people as a rule motor down to the spot selected, sending their servants down beforehand to make all arrangements. They then prefer to wait on each other, and the servants to make themselves scarce.'[29]

The sixty menus for light, sophisticated meals set out in Hilda Leyel's *Picnics for Motorists* (1936) include mousse of haddock, cold Welsh neck of mutton and mint sauce, macedoine of vegetables, cream cheese and caraway rolls. Hot soup or even ice cream, in other menus, was carried in special wide-mouthed 'Thermos' flasks. Unbreakable 'Betelware' cups and saucers were recommended, and suggested beverages were bottled beer, wine, cider or lemonade.[30]

Nineteenth-century picnickers, already amply supplied with other food, would occasionally boil a few potatoes over a wood fire as a romantic, gipsy-style entertainment.[31] Sportsmen might reheat a ready-made stew on 'a little wood fire in a sheltered corner' at a shooting picnic on a cold day.[32] Later the concept of open-air cookery became more familiar through the Boy Scout and Girl Guide movements, whose camp food was both cooked and eaten out of doors. On family picnics children gathered twigs and their fathers made fires on which to boil the tea-kettle.

The influential cookery writer Elizabeth David was a keen picnicker. A friend recalled several London picnics shared with her in a square behind the Guildhall Library, where they worked together in the mid-1970s gathering notes for her bread book. A planted area in the centre of the square surrounded a small pool, and there Elizabeth would plunge the bottle of white wine, securing it with string to an overhanging bush. After their morning's work the two would emerge to lay out rugs and tablecloth and enjoy home-baked bread, butter, cheese, a *Tian* and fruit with the well-chilled wine.[33]

Like picnic food, street food, too, has changed considerably over the years. Early in the twentieth century it still followed Victorian patterns, consisting of pies and pasties, fish and chips eaten from newspaper bundles,[34] fruit, and ice cream sold from barrows, and later tricycles. However, food sold on the street disappeared temporarily during both world wars. In the 1960s came spit-roasted chicken, portions of which were carved off and sold together with separate bags of stuffing. Since then the plethora of new packaging materials such as polystyrene has widened the scope of what can be eaten in the street, and numerous confections from foreign cuisine – risotto, paella, curry, etc. – are on sale in take-away form. Snacking has now become a way of life, among younger people especially; they can be seen in the streets eating takeaways and drinking cola and other such beverages from cans at all hours of the day and night.

The very last word shall go to a much-celebrated outdoor meal of our time. Around the lake at North London's Kenwood the picnic can be observed in every conceivable form – from the most sophisticated (table and chairs, damask cloth, silverware and elaborately served dishes) to the most simple (a rug and a few sandwiches) – during the supper interval in the summertime open-air concert season.

The millennium picnic basket shown opposite would not be out of place there.

FIG. 93
A Picnic for the Millennium, photographed on location at Kenwood House, Hampstead

This millennium picnic reflects many aspects of today's British food and design but at the same time expresses something of the traditional flavour of alfresco eating. The multi-ethnic mixture of sushi, hummus and onion bahjis sits alongside champagne, ripe figs, exotic fruit and strawberries, as well as pork pies and Stilton cheese. The three themes of innovation, celebration and tradition befitting an exploration of food at the brink of the twenty-first century are equally apparent in the array of picnic- and tableware – a mix of individual modern studio pieces and some of the latest commercially available factory-produced bowls and dishes. The use of traditional techniques in a modern context can be seen in the plaited, twined, coiled and lashed stainless steel dish by Dail Behennah. Employing conventional basketmaking methods of construction, it uses stainless steel rope, more usually found in heavy industrial lifting gear, to create a strikingly modern platter. Conversely, the same maker employs traditional basketry materials to stunning effect in 'Coiled Form', the elegant cane dish at the centre of the photograph. Similarly, Debbie Booth's highly-coloured willow basket is a reworking of the traditional picnic hamper. However, it is made from willow grown as a locally sourced sustainable resource without the use of dyestuffs. There are three types of unpeeled willow, giving orange, green and brown, while the white willow is simply stripped of its bark. The buff is boiled and then stripped, the tannin in the bark giving this willow its distinctive colour, whereas the black willow is achieved by boiling but not stripping. Some of these same environmental concerns can be seen in the very different aesthetic of Lois Walpole's picnic basket made from juice cartons (see also figs 94 & 95). This uses 100% recycled materials woven together to create a highly imaginative work. The outer basket folds out, forming a picnic rug and revealing the brightly-coloured main basket. This cylindrical section in two parts contains plates, glasses and cutlery also made from recycled materials. The theme of millennial celebration is taken up by the magnum-size silver champagne-cooler and parcel gilt goblets from the 'Celebration' range by Asprey & Garrard. Designed in-house and bearing the firm's own mark, they are also hallmarked with the special Millennium Mark. A very different 'take' on the same theme can be seen in Kate Malone's 'Millennium Mug', which uses traditional applied decorative motifs, while the exotic fruit available to today's supermarket shopper is represented by her pineapple jug. This thickly glazed crystalline stoneware contrasts with the cool elegance of the white porcelain bowls produced by the studio potter Hilary Roberts, whose individual shapes in turn contrast with the factory-produced uniformity of plates from Royal Doulton's simple, modernistic 'Fusion' range.

FIGS 94 & 95
Picnic basket made by Lois Walpole (b.1952) from woven recycled juice cartons, 1999
Height: 62 cm Width: 85 cm Depth: 85 cm

The millennium picnic basket specially commissioned for the exhibition which this book accompanies uses 100% recycled materials. Both the outer basket – which folds out to form a picnic rug – and the brightly-coloured main basket are made from woven and stitched fruit-juice cartons that have been cut into long continuous strips. The cylindrical inner basket contains a selection of picnic plates, bowls, cutlery and tumblers that are also made from recycled materials, such as plastic bottles.

The concept was to create a radically modern interpretation of the traditional picnic basket, using recycled materials for both environmental and aesthetic reasons. Liberating the maker from the preconceptions associated with conventional materials, this novel use of waste packaging enabled Lois Walpole to experiment freely to produce an imaginative, colourful and striking reworking of a traditional form.

CHAPTER 6

A Meal for the Millennium

WE ARE all familiar with the vast increase in Britain's population during the nineteenth century and the great exodus of people from the country as they set off in search of work in the rapidly expanding industrial towns. In 1801 four-fifths of the population lived in the country, but a century later the same large proportion were living in towns. Traditionally most people had lived close to the land, their livelihood largely dependent on agriculture and handicraft and their daily life and diet linked closely to the cycle of the seasons, festivals and holy days. Since climate, custom and proclivity varied from place to place, and there was no national transport system to spread localized habits further afield, food was not only seasonal but also markedly regional.

The industrial revolution changed all this, and a social and physical transformation of Britain came about inexorably during the nineteenth century. The fact that the nation had become predominantly urbanized was no cause for regret on the part of the many sections of the population whose standard of living and life expectancy continued steadily to improve. At the same time, large numbers of the new urban working class were living in wretched poverty, but the lot of the country labourer was often no better.

The problem of feeding so many town dwellers was partially solved by a series of discoveries made in the last twenty-five years or so of the nineteenth century. The principle of pasteurization, the invention of roller-milling, the refrigeration of steamships carrying cheap frozen meat from the New World, the improved process of canning and the factory production of cheese and margarine were vital advances, well established by the early years of the twentieth century. Indispensable to the supply of provisions was the expansion of the railways. Food was no longer provided largely from local sources; its distribution became a far more national enterprise, and the regionalism of the British diet began to decline.

Industrialism is indifferent to the natural boundaries of family, class, region and nation. Ignoring tradition and local custom, its essential drive is towards ever greater efficiency via uniformity and economies of scale. On the other hand, what we may call the domestic principle entails an altogether different order of priorities. It is governed by need and relies on tradition, with values of homeliness and generosity overriding those of speed and efficiency. Contrasting the twentieth-century dominance of the industrial over the domestic, in 1945 Flora Thompson described the making of an invalid jelly:

> *Few would care to take the time and trouble in these days... On the face of it, it does seem a waste of time to spend the inside of a week making a small jelly, and women were soon to have other uses for their time and energy, but those who did such cookery...looked upon it as an art, and no time or trouble was thought wasted if the result were perfection.*[1]

With similar preoccupations in mind, even before the 1860s, when Augusta Llanover wrote *The First Principles of Good Cookery*, a few had set about recording regional foods in an attempt to salvage Britain's fast-disappearing culinary traditions.[2]

Linked to the burgeoning of the Victorian middle classes, an unsavoury alliance developed between the prevailing tenets of thrift and economy and the confused belief that only complicated (French-style) food was good. Aping the few in Britain who kept fine tables, served by gifted chefs from abroad, a bastardized version of *haute cuisine* was created by the bourgoisie, within whose ambit appearance rather than taste reigned supreme. Hence, at the end of the nineteenth century, in socially ambitious circles the prevailing attitude towards plain and simply cooked food had become one of conditioned snobbery.

During the first half of the twentieth century writers such as Florence White,[3] Moreton Shand[4] and later Dorothy Hartley[5] carried on the task begun by Augusta Llanover by encouraging the English to understand their own traditions, now lost to all but a few. In founding the English Folk Cookery Association in the 1930s, Florence White's aim was to record the living remnants of Britain's culinary heritage before the industrialization of food completely crushed it out of existence.

After the First World War fewer young working-class women were prepared to go into domestic service, and after the Second World War there was even greater reluctance, so those women who had previously employed servants were left with no alternative but to learn how to cook for themselves. The less well-off woman had fared little better; through the dislocations of war and rationing, she had been deprived of the opportunity to learn culinary skills from her mother or grandmother. Despite the popularity at all levels of post-war cookery classes, women's magazines and later the television cook, cookery remained entrenched in the collective mind as a chore.

As to eating out, since the nineteenth century this habit had grown in popularity among the better-off, becoming seen as more than an occasional necessity while on long journeys. Meanwhile, the best restaurateurs had been imported, largely from France, and with them new attitudes to food. Two such representatives who, at the turn of the century, had helped consolidate eating out as an acceptable and fashionable pastime were César Ritz and Auguste Escoffier.[6] If somewhat modified in scale, this minority entertainment continued after the Second World War, although at a wider level the national diet was still indomitably British. Certain powerful forces, however, were poised to bring about a rapid democratization of the British way of eating.

Rationing was finally lifted in the mid-1950s and for some time afterwards the prosperity of the country continued to grow. This new-found affluence encouraged the less than wealthy to adopt two radically new ways of eating – taking advantage of the processed, labour-saving foods now flooding the market, and eating outside the home. The emergence of these trends coincided with large numbers of immigrants arriving in Britain from China, India and the Middle East, bringing with them influences from three of the world's major cuisines.

Italian immigrants, some of whom had settled in Britain before the First World War, constituted one ethnic minority group that had already established a small culinary foothold for itself with family-run cafés. Nonetheless, it was post-war Chinese immigrants who came to dominate the bottom end of the restaurant trade. The initial popularity of their establishments had little to do with appreciation of Chinese cooking as such, but was founded above all on the fact that they served cheap, fast food. The only other immigrant community presenting any serious competition to this monopoly during the 1960s and '70s, was that from the Indian subcontinent. By the 1980s Greek-Cypriot and Turkish proprietors were opening restaurants in competition with the Chinese and Indians, while American-style fast-food chains were blazing their way through the high streets of towns throughout the land.

Cooking and baking at home was already in decline before the war, and with the advent of first canned foods, then frozen and most recently cook-chilled, the drift away from home cooking towards convenience foods has continued steadily over the past fifty years. The generation of women who had worked during the war on the whole returned to their domestic roles afterwards. However, by the 1960s many of their daughters were choosing to remain at work after marriage. Since this left them with less time for cooking at home, ready-made foods of one kind or another were utilized to produce meals with greater speed and efficiency.

As the food companies continued to expand, the very nature of food shopping was changing beyond all recognition. Passing on reductions in overheads to the customer in the form of lower prices, the self-service store had been launched in America during the 1930s. At the end of the 1940s Jack Cohen's Tesco stores were among the first shops in Britain to offer this new service. The stores grew both in number and size to become, by the 1960s, the much larger and more aptly named supermarkets.

Neither the astonishing rise in the use of convenience foods in Britain nor the technological and manufacturing revolution that brought it about would have been possible without an unprecedented set of mechanical developments in the post-war period. A rash of labour-saving domestic appliances that were aggressively promoted quickly became perceived as necessities for both those recently servantless and those newly affluent. Important among these was the refrigerator, but even more vital to the use of modern convenience foods, since the 1970s, has been the wholesale acceptance of the domestic freezer and the microwave oven. In combination, these appliances have made it possible to construct entire meals with pre-cooked or processed food that can be heated up and served in minutes.

After the war probably the single most influential person writing in reaction to the bleak English culinary climate was Elizabeth David. Valiantly attempting to lift Britain out of the trough into which it had fallen, she encouraged her readers to strive for something better. Taken up at first only by a privileged minority, her ideas gradually extended to the aspiring young professionals of the middle classes.[7] Under her influence they turned away from what was seen as an impoverished British tradition and began to take their inspiration from abroad. It is interesting to observe that, with Elizabeth David in the vanguard, most of the best cookery writers of the next generation – such as Claudia Roden,[8] Alan Davidson,[9] Jane Grigson[10] and Madhur Jaffrey[11] – were notable not only for their proposal of the same culinary principles, but also for a similar lack of formal training.

So, too, have those British restaurants that have recognized the essential features and attitudes common to *all* good cooking in many instances been run by gifted and dedicated amateurs, operating on a small scale. Their chefs have rarely graduated from either the conventional French *haute cuisine* or the unimaginative mainstream British catering training routes.

The reciprocal effects of private and public eating habits is difficult to gauge. Nevertheless, the interrelationship between the better cookery writers, their increasingly widely travelled readership and like-minded restaurateurs undoubtedly helped create a small but growing mentality of discernment in Britain as the readers of the cookery books ate out at restaurants, whose owners were themselves devotees of the books.

Despite these improvements, it would be unrealistic to claim that the spread of Elizabeth David's ethos, further extended by her younger counterparts, has had an impact on more than a fraction of the population. Indeed, much public and private food in Britain is every bit as bad, and in some cases pretentious, now as it was fifty years ago. In addition, during these same fifty years home cooking has declined, and many families eat ready-prepared and synthetic foods of one kind or another. Meanwhile, British caterers ruthlessly exploit the growing trend towards eating out. A variety of fast-food chains serve processed, denatured 'comfort food' of a mind-numbing predictability. For more affluent sections of society, preoccupied with 'lifestyle', a growing number of restaurants indulge their penchant for food as conspicuous display rather than integrity of taste.

In the light of our understanding of the industrial promise of progressively easy, efficient and convenient food, we are in a position to take stock. We have experienced the standardization inherent in mass production as well as the packaging and gimmickry masquerading as variety, which enables us to recognize that at the dawn of the new millennium we are actually presented with less genuine variety and quality. Growing concern as to the environmental effects of high-yield fertilizer and pesticide production, and the consequent purity and quality of our nutrition, is amply reflected in just two examples of ongoing preoccupation: BSE in cattle and genetically engineered food. The net result is a pervasive disillusionment, unease and sense of powerlessness in the face of corporate technology and mass-produced food.

Food is never far from anyone's thoughts, and until now people have found it not only useful but also beneficial to their well-being to practise its production, preservation and cooking with the greatest ingenuity and skill. The knowledge and expertise required to make good food, which has long been perceived as more than just a simple necessity of life, has been celebrated and prized almost as much as the successful cultivation and harvesting of crops. Our elemental relationship with food is linked traditionally with the daily thanksgiving for existence and has long been reiterated through the cycle of the seasons and the various stages of family and community life. In accepting the blandness, questionable methods and ultimately diminished choice that are concomitant with the mass production and distribution of food, we reject the kitchen and thus forfeit our culinary skills. Rather than liberating ourselves, as we believe, we may in truth be settling for diminished standards – and do so at our peril.

Yet, in an overwhelmingly industrial society, even with the very best of intentions it is extremely difficult to eat food that is not purveyed via mass production and high-profile consumer marketing. Agribusiness, intensive animal-rearing, factory processing and supermarket distribution are the structures upon which our nutrition is based. Nevertheless, more people are now making their own contribution to improving the beleaguered state of our eating habits. Whether at home or eating out, they show far more appreciation and knowledge of food than they did in previous years.

Cooking is no longer essential, and as a consequence it is not these days always seen as mere drudgery. Those for whom cookery is a leisure activity approach it with a more experimental yet discerning attitude of mind; different cuisines and styles are explored and perfected, often with considerable skill. Unlike most other countries, in Britain most traditional dishes have gradually fallen out of use with the industrialization of our diet. At the turn of the millennium we are responding to a variety of forces and creating for ourselves an astonishingly varied cuisine.

Britain has changed irreversibly since the Second World War. Yet, in regretting our losses, we would do well both to remember the gains and to remain cautious about romanticizing the past. With time, and a deeper understanding of the irreplaceable virtues of seasonal foods produced by dedicated local producers, perhaps we will fully appreciate Elizabeth David's reflections on the subject of English food:

> *We need to go back to the recipes of more than a century ago to the early and mid-nineteenth century, when an authentic and strong English cooking tradition flourished.*[12]

FIG. 96
Place setting 2000

This modern table setting features a tall, exotic champagne flute designed by David Redman for Royal Brierley. The champagne is being chilled in a marvellously robust Dartington ice pail, which takes its inspiration from the earlier verrières of the Regency period. The design of the shallow plates by Nick Munro returns us full circle to the flat roundels or trenchers of the Tudor period. At the same time, Michael Hjort's elegant dish – dariole of salmon tartare on cucumber with langoustine– reminds us of those principles of freshness and simplicity advocated by Elizabeth David that have had such a profound influence on British food over the past forty years. The setting is complemented by Lucien Taylor's ergonomic 'new wave' silver cutlery and his witty gilded bon-bon dishes.

Photographic Credits

Front cover Guildhall Library, Corporation of London; back cover Norfolk Museums Service (Norwich Castle Museum); frontispiece Jeremy Philips for Fairfax House, York; figs 1, 10, 30, 41, 66, 71, 74, 82, 83, 94 & 95 Norfolk Museums Service (Norwich Castle Museum); fig. 2 Ashmolean Museum, Oxford; figs 3 & 22 Nev Taylor for Fairfax House, York; figs 4, 5 & 6 Hatfield House, Hertfordshire, UK/Bridgeman Art Library; figs 9, 61, 75, 78 & 89 Tate Gallery Photographic Department; fig. 11 Harrogate Museums and Art Gallery, UK/Bridgeman Art Library; fig. 12 Guildhall Art Gallery, Corporation of London, UK/Bridgeman Art Library; fig. 13 Private Collection/Bridgeman Art Library; figs 14, 15, 16, 17, 27, 33 & 39 Guildhall Library, Corporation of London; figs 20, 21, 24, 26, 31, 35, 46, 49, 70, 72, 73 & 96 Jeremy Phillips for Fairfax House, York; figs 23, 25 & 43 Ivan Day; figs 28 & 29 David Howard; fig. 32 © Colin Self 2000 All rights reserved DACS; figs 34, 42, 53, 58, 59, 60 & 77 The Royal Collection © Her Majesty Queen Elizabeth II; fig. 36 © Crown Copyright NMR; fig. 37 Devonshire Collection, Bolton Hall. By permission of the Duke of Devonshire and the Chatsworth Settlement Trustees; fig. 38 Longleat House, Wiltshire, UK/Bridgeman Art Library; fig. 40 Gavin Mist for Fairfax House, York; figs 44 & 45 Minton Museum, Stoke-on-Trent; fig. 47 MMD – Museen des Mobiliendepots – Wien; fig. 48 Brotherton Library, Leeds; figs 50 & 92 Bradford Art Galleries and Museums; fig. 51 Sheffield Galleries and Museums Trust, UK/Bridgeman Art Library; fig. 52 Manchester City Art Galleries; fig. 54 Abegg-Stiftung, Riggisberg (Chr. Von Virag); figs 55, 56 & 57 Broadfield House Glass Museum; fig. 62 By courtesy of the Trustees of Sir John Soane's Museum; fig. 63 Private Collection/Bridgeman Art Library; fig. 64 Private Collection, courtesy of First Site at the Minories; fig. 65 City of Plymouth Museums & Art Gallery; fig. 68 Bradford Art Galleries and Museums, UK/Bridgeman Art Library © Courtesy of the artist's estate/Bridgeman Art Library; fig. 69 By courtesy of the National Portrait Gallery, London; fig. 76 Sotheby's, London; fig. 79 Board of Trustees of the National Museums and Galleries on Merseyside (Walker Art Gallery, Liverpool); fig. 80 Bradford Art Galleries and Museums, UK/Bridgeman Art Library; fig. 81 Private Collection; fig. 84 Russell-Cotes Art Gallery and Museum, Bournemouth; fig. 85 Museum of London (D527); fig. 87 John Roan; fig. 88 Torre Abbey, Torquay, Devon, UK/Bridgeman Art Library; fig. 90 Royal Scottish Academy (Diploma Collection); fig. 91 Viscount Windsor; fig. 93 Nigel Corrie for English Heritage.

Notes & References

CHAPTER 1:

1. Thomas Moufet, *Healths Improvement*, London 1633, p.272.
2. Edward Hake, *Newes out of Powles Churchyard*, London 1579, Dii, Diii.
3. William Salmon, *The New London Dispensatory*, London 1690, pp.222–3.
4. W.M., *The Queens Closet Open'd* , London 1655.
5. Francis Deloney, *Jack of Newbury*, London 1633.
6. J. Nichols, *Progresses and Public Processions of James I*, London 1828.
7. Revd Stodherd Abdy, 'A Journal of a Visit into Berkshire, 1770', in A. A. Houblon, *The Houblon Family*, London, Constable, vol. 2; anonymous poem in *St. James's Chronicle*, 1799, VI, 16–18 April; G. Oliver, 'Old Christmas customs and popular superstitions of Lincolnshire', *Gentleman's Magazine*, CII, 1832, pp.491–4.
8. Robert May, *The Accomplisht Cook*, 3rd edition, London 1685, pp.234–5.
9. Isabella Beeton, *The Book of Household Management*, London 1861.
10. Elizabeth Raffald, *The Experienced English Housekeeper*, London 1769.
11. *Letters of Lady Rachel Russell*, London 1773, p.105.
12. John Harland (ed.), *The Home and Farm Accounts of the Shuttleworths of Gawthorpe*, Chetham Society, 1868, vol. 1, p.2/2.
13. John Nott, *The Cook's and Confectioner's Dictionary*, London 1723, C188.
14. Reginald Wilenski, *John Ruskin*, London 1933,
15. W.P. Frith, *My Autobiography and Reminiscences*, London 1887.
16. John Brand, *Observations on Popular Antiquities*, London 1807, vol. II, p.193.
17. Mr Hunt, 21 October 1830, manuscript letter in Alderman Sir John Key Collection, Guildhall Library, London.
18. Francis Sandford, *History of the Coronation of James II*, London 1687.
19. The painting remained unfinished and was later misattributed until its recent reappraisal by Vivien Knight of the Guildhall Art Gallery.
20. Elias Ashmole, *Institutions, Laws and Ceremonies of the Most Noble Order of the Garter*, London 1672, pp.588–607.
21. Sandford, as cited in note 18.
22. Wynken de Worde, *The Boke of Kervynge*, London 1508.
23. In Naples ices were evolving at this time into light and sophisticated delicacies flavoured with a remarkable range of ingredients, including chocolate, candied pumpkin and pinenut milk. In England, however, even at the sovereign's table the first English ices were likely to have been a dense frozen mass of sweetened cream, probably scented with orange-flower water.

CHAPTER 2:

1. Gervase Markham, *The English Housewife*, London 1615.
2. Girolamo Ruscelli, *The Secretes of Maister Alexis of Piedmont*, London 1558.
3. Hugh Platt, *Delights for Ladies*, London 1600.
4. John Murrell, *A Daily Exercise for Ladies and Gentlewomen*, London 1617.
5. Emerson, *English Traits*, 1856.
6. Isabella Beeton, *The Book of Household Management*, London 1861.
7. Markham, as cited in note 1.
8. John Nott, *The Cook's and Confectioner's Dictionary*, London 1723.
9. Markham, as cited in note 1.
10. William Kitchener, *The Cook's Oracle*, London 1823.
11. Ibid.
12. Philip Stubbes, *Anatomie of Abuses*, London 1583.
13. C. Shuckman, & D. de Hoop Scheffer, *Dutch and Flemish Etchings, Engravings and Woodcuts* c.*1450–1700*, Rosendal 1991, vol. XXXVIII, p.10. We are grateful to Christopher Pringle for drawing our attention to the Vischer etching.
14. Lucy Aikin, *Memoirs of the Court of Queen Elizabeth*, London 1819, p.274.
15. Ivan Day, 'Sculpture for the Eighteenth Century Garden Dessert', in Harlan Walker (ed.), *Food in the Arts*, Prospect Books, 1999.
16. Bartolomeo Scappi, *Opera*, Venice 1570.
17. Murrell, as cited in note 4.
18. Charles Estienne, *Maison Rustique, or the Countrey Farme. Compyled in the French Tongue by Charles Stevens and John Liebault, and translated into English by Richard Surfleet. Reviewed, corrected and augmented by Gervase Markham*, London 1616.
19. John Parkinson, *Theatrum Botanicum*, London 1640.
20. Kitchener, as cited in note 10.

21. William Puttenham, *The Art of English Poesie*, London 1589.
22. Peter Brown & Ivan Day, *The Pleasures of the Table*, York 1997.
23. Anthony Wells-Cole, *Art and Decoration in Elizabethan and Jacobean England*, USA, Yale University Press, 1997, p.23.
24. Robert Raines, *Marcellus Laroon*, London 1967.
25. *The Whole Duty of a Woman*, London 1737.
26. R. Holinshed, *Chronicles*, vol. I: *The Description and Historie of England written by W.H.*, London 1587, p.168.
27. Markham, as cited in note 1.
28. F. White, *Good Things*, Jonathan Cape, London 1932, p.72.
29. Markham, as cited in note 1, p.241.
30. Tobias Smollett, *The Expedition of Humphry Clinker*, 1771: Everyman edition, ed. Peter Miles, London, J.M. Dent, 1993, p.249.
31. C. Anne Wilson, *Food and Drink in Britain*, London, Constable, 1991, p.261.
32. Estienne, as cited in note 18.
33. William Ellis, *The Country Housewife's Family Companion*, London 1750, p.75.
34. J. Woodforde, *Diary of a Country Parson 1758–1802*, passages selected and edited by John Beresford, Oxford, Oxford University Press.
35. Alfred Peacock, *Bread and Blood*, London, Victor Gollancz, 1965, p.14.
36. Flora Thompson, *Lark Rise to Candleford*, London, Guild Books, 1946, p.216.
37. Ibid., p.217.
38. Horace Walpole, *Correspondence*, Yale edition, New Haven, Conn., 1941.
39. J.H. Plumb, *The First Four Georges*, p.152.
40. It is estimated that the Prince spent £450,000 on Carlton House and £750,000 on the Brighton Pavilion.
41. Lyttelton correspondence, 103–4.
42. Christie's, The Duke of York's Sale, 19–22 March 1827.
43. Royal Archives (RA) 26329–31.
44. RA 26333.
45. RA 26330.
46. P.R.O. HO73/18 – 1794.
47. Brown & Day, as cited in note 22, p.28.
48. G. de Bellaigue, *Sèvres Porcelain in the collection of Her Majesty the Queen*, 1986.
49. RA 25133.
50. RA 25191.
51. RA 25276 and 25317.
52. RA 25328.
53. Carlton House Catalogue, 1991, p.17
54. RA 25200.
55. RA 26395.
56. RA 26377.
57. RA 26390.
58. Farrington, p.2745.
59. RA 26284–92.
60. Carlton House Catalogue (as cited in note 53) and *Princes as Patrons* Catalogue, 1998, pp.106–8.
61. RA 26428:

Altering the plateau to receive the above, new feet, etc. gilded metal frames and new plinth	£130.0.0d.
Gilding ditto all over in the best manner dead and red	£428.0.0d.

62. RA 26290.
63. This topic will form part of a major exhibition at Fairfax House, York in 2002.
64. RA 26404, illustrated in *Princes as Patrons* Catalogue, p.113, pl.111.
65. RA 26403.
66. *Annual Register*, vol. 53, 1811, p.68.
67. These may relate to the chinoiserie decorations provided by Catherine – see RA 26395.
68. Ch. Colchester (ed.), *The Diaries and Correspondence of Charles Abbot, Lord Colchester* (II) 19 June 1811, p.61. See also p.338 (Lord Tierney) and *Gentleman's Magazine*, June 1811, p.536.
69. RA, Carlton House ledgers, 1812–21.
70. Antonin Carème worked in England from 1815 to 1818.
71. Carlton House Ledgers, as cited in note 69.

TOTALS CONSUMED

Beef	Mutton	Veal	
627	97	546	
40 Heart sweetbreads		Butter	216

18 Necks house lamb		Eggs	10 × 100
4 Shoulder of		Bacon	167
		Lard	51
22 Pullets		Cream	40
14 large Capons		Double	34
102 Chickens		Milk	4
12 Guinea Fowls		Bd sugar	44
6 Pea Fowls		Trebled "	47
24 Fowls		Currants	12
2 Ragout		Raisans	12
4 Combs		Lisb sugar	12
		Almonds	24
16 Lobsters		Buttered "	1
8 Soles		Mace	8
300 Crayfish		Cloves	8
500 Prawns		Nutmeg	4
		Hams	279¾
		Tongues	37
		Gerkins	2
		Rice	12
		Vermicilly	4
		Scotthein do	1
		Anchivoes	10
		Capers	12
		Maccaroni	2
Port	17	Cayenne	2
Sherry	24	Pepper	2
Claret	3	Isinglass	2
Madeira	6	Oil	6
Champin	2	Mustard	6
Brandy	2	Salt	1

72. RA, Coronation Banquet, 19 July 1821.
73. C. Hibbert, *George IV*, 1975, p.195.
74. Ibid.
75. Murdie, R., *A Historical Account of His Majesty's visit to Scotland*, Edinburgh 1822.
76. Ibid., p.230.
77. Ibid., p.233.
78. Ibid., pp.234–42.
79. RA 25407. For a discussion of these types of mobile, see Brown & Schwartz, *Come Drink the Bowl Dry*, 1996, pp.80–9.
80. Hibbert, as cited in note 73, p.327.
81. Ibid.
82. Ibid., p.345.

CHAPTER 3:

1. *Northumberland Household Book. The Regulations and Establishment of the Household of Henry Algernon Percy... 1512*, new edition, 1905.
2. *A Collection of Ordinances and Regulations for the Government of the Royal Households, made in Divers Reigns*, London, Society of Antiquaries, 1790.
3. Gervase Markham, *The English Housewife*, London 1615.
4. Quoted in John Bickerdyke, *The Curiosities of Ale and Beer*, London 1889.
5. William Buchan, *Domestic Medicine*, London 1803.
6. Norman Scarfe (tr. & ed.), *A Frenchman's Year in Suffolk 1784*, Woodbridge, Boydell (Suffolk Records Society, vol. 30), 1988, pp.21–2.
7. *The Déjeuné; or, Companion for the Breakfast Table* (Published every morning, etc.), vol. 1, London 1820; *Dry Toast, prepared for the Sunday morning breakfast*, nos 1–3, London 1823.
8. Frederick Nutt, *The Compleat Confectioner*, London 1789.
9. Nicholas Breton, *Fantasticks*, 1626, 22: The 12 Houres; see Alexander B. Grossart (ed.), *The Works in Verse and Prose of Nicholas Breton*, Chertsey Worthies Library, 1879, vol. 2, section 1, pp.12–15. The porridge pot was on for the servants' breakfast during the third hour of the day.
10. *The Closet of the Eminently Learned Sir Kenelme Digby. Kt. Opened*, London 1671, p.134. Recipe for Pan Cotto: 'A wholesome course of diet is, to eat one of these, or Panada, or Cream of Oatmeal, or Barley, or two Newlaid eggs for breakfast... Two poched eggs with a few fine dry fryed Collops of pure Bacon, are not bad for breakfast, or to begin a meal.'
11. *The Court and Kitchen of Elizabeth commonly called Joan Cromwell*, London 1664, p.56: 'How to make Marrow Puddings, (which she usually had to her Breakfast.).' The ingredients are: '1 lbs of ground Jordan almonds, Rosewater, 1 lbs of sugar, a grated penny loaf, nutmeg, 1 pint of cream, the marrow from two marrowbones, Ambergris and salt, stuffed into skins.'
12. For breakfasts of about 1800 see Eileen White, 'Breakfast with Jane Austen', in *Petits Propos Culinaires* 47, Prospect Books, August 1994, 43–7.
13. *The Breakfast Book*, London 1865.
14. Ibid., p.vi.
15. Isabella Beeton, *The Book of Household Management*, London 1861, p.939, paras 2144–6.
16. Beeton (1880), pp.1233–4.
17. Frederick Bishop, *The Wife's Own Book of Cookery*, London 1862, pp.32–3.
18. Major L..., *Breakfasts, Luncheons, and Ball Suppers*, London 1887, p.2. (The author has been identified as Major James Henry Landon.)
19. B. Seebohm Rowntree, *Poverty: A Study of Town Life*, London 1901, p.281.

CHAPTER 4:

1. *New Zealand Listener*, 22 Nov. 1957, 4:3.
2. C. Anne Wilson, *Food and Drink in Britain* 19, p.414.
3. W.H. Ukers, *All About Tea*, London 1935.
4. 1660 Pepys Diary, 25 September.
5. Thomas Garway, *An Exact Description of the Growth, Quality, and Vertues of the Leaf Tee, alias Tay*, London 1660.
6. Henry Stubbes, *The Natural History of Coffee, Thee, Chocolate and Tobacco*, London 1682.
7. William Salmon, *The Family Dictionary*, London 1710.
8. Ibid.
9. *The Women's Petition against Coffee*, London n.d., *c.*1674.
10. Thomas Tryon, *The Good House-wife made a Doctor*, London 1692.
11. Quoted by Mrs Delany in *Life & Correspondence*, London 1861, I.172.
12. Wilson, as cited in note 2, p.413.
13. Salmon, as cited in note 7.
14. Revd Stodherd Abdy, 'A Journal of a Visit into Berkshire, 1770', in A.A. Houblon, *The Houblon Family*, London 1907.
15. William Cobbett, *Cottage Economy*, London 1820.
16. William Buchan, *Observations concerning the Diet of the Common People*, London 1797.
17. Ibid.
18. Ibid.
19. Wilson, as cited in note 2, p.417.
20. Laura Mason, 'Everything Stops for Tea', in C. Anne Wilson (ed.), *Luncheon, Nuncheon and Other Meals*, Stroud, Alan Sutton Publishing Ltd, 1994.
21. Isabella Beeton, *The Book of Household Management*, London 1892, p.1440.
22. Ibid.
23. L. Irvine, *Royal Doulton Bunnykins Collectors' Book*, Richard Dennis, London 1984.

CHAPTER 5:

1. Posidonius, quoted by Athenæus and Diodorus (his original book has not survived): see J.J. Tierney, *The Celtic Ethnography of Posidonius*, 1960, 60C, pp.247, 250.
2. George Turberville's *Book of Faulconrie*, 1575 (facsimile reprint), Oxford 1908, p.123.
3. For more information on both aspects, see C. Anne Wilson (ed.), *Banquetting Stuffe: the Fare and Social Background of the Tudor and Stuart Banquet*, Edinburgh 1991.
4. See C. Anne Wilson (ed.), *Luncheon, Nuncheon and Other Meals*, Stroud 1994, pp.34–6. By then 'nuncheon' was a dialect word in Yorkshire and Wiltshire.
5. Ibid., p.41.
6. William Ellis, *The Country Housewife's Family Companion*, London 1750, p.76.
7. Peter Brears, *Traditional Food in Yorkshire*, Edinburgh 1987, p.52.

8. P. Earle, *A City full of People*, London 1994, pp.223–4
9. Brompton Park was founded in 1681; see M. Thick, *The Neat House Gardens*, Totnes, Prospect Books, 1998, pp.59, 129–30.
10. D. Solkin, 'Vauxhall Gardens', in his *Painting for Money*, New Haven, Conn. 1995, p.157.
11. Tea-drinking and the ritual of its preparation were introduced at Court by Catherine of Braganza, wife of King Charles II.
12. E.B. Chancellor, *The Eighteenth Century in London*, London 1920, pp.102–4.
13. Horace Walpole, *Correspondence*, Yale edition, New Haven, Conn. 1941, vol. 9, p.109.
14. Samuel Pepys, *The Diary of Samuel Pepys*, ed. Robert Latham & William Matthews, London 1970–83, entry for 6 July 1664; see also 9 April 1661.
15. G. Battiscombe, *English Picnics*, London 1949, pp.5–8.
16. Jane Austen, *Pride and Prejudice*, 1815, vol. 2, chapter 16. N. Edgeworth, 'The Absentee', in her *Tales of Fashionable Life*, 1812, vol. 6, chapter 6.
17. John Montagu, 4th Earl of Sandwich once passed 24 hours thus, sustained only by beef sandwiches; see *Oxford English Dictionary*, 2nd edition, 1989, vol. 14.
18. Jane Austen, *Emma*, chapter 42; Charles Dickens, *The Pickwick Papers*, chapter 19.
19. See p.107. High tea, a later and larger meal, developed in Scotland and the North of England and worked its way south. See Laura Mason, 'Everything Stops for Tea', in *Luncheon, Nuncheon* (cited in note 4), pp.82–90.
20. Charlotte Brontë, *Shirley*, chapter 17.
21. *Cries of York*, York, Kendrew, *c.*1820, pp.8, 18, 21, 23.
22. Henry Mayhew, *The Morning Chronicle Survey of Labour and the Poor*, new edition, London 1980, vol. 1, pp.249, 265–7. Fried chipped potatoes were sold, without fish, in the 1860s in northern industrial towns; see J.K. Walton, *Fish and Chips and the British Working Class, 1870-1940*, Leicester 1992, pp.25–6.
23. Anthony Trollope, *Can You Forgive Her?*, chapter 8.
24. Francis Kilvert, *Diary*, selections, ed. W. Plomer, London 1977, vol. 3, p.427 (16 October 1878).
25. Mireille Galinou, 'Towards Respectability: Tissot's Picnics', *Country Life*, 13 July 1989.
26. Olive M. Geddes, *The Laird's Kitchen*, Edinburgh 1994, p.96 (National Library of Scotland MS.24777, f.8.5).
27. Major L..., *Breakfasts, Luncheons and Ball Suppers*, London 1887, pp.40, 51. For a menu for a picnic for forty persons, see Isabella Beeton, *The Book of Household Management*, 1861, reprinted in facsimile several times, p.960, sections 2149–50.
28. F. Jack, *The Woman's Book*, London 1911, p.344.
29. Ibid.
30. Mrs C.F. Leyel, *Picnics for Motorists*, London 1936, p.2 and menu no. 27.
31. Kilvert, as cited in note 24, vol. 1, pp.161–2 (21 June 1870).
32. A. Kenney Herbert, *Picnics and Suppers*, London 1901, p.248.
33. A. Boyes, in J. Norman. (ed.), *South Wind through the Kitchen*, London 1997, pp.54–5. A *Tian* is a Provençal 'gratin of green vegetables' with olive oil and additions of fish, eggs, etc.; see Elizabeth David, *A Book of Mediterranean Food*, Penguin, 1955, p.160 for recipe. The wine was never removed by other hands.
34. With minimal greaseproof paper between the food and the newsprint.

CHAPTER 6:

1. Flora Thompson, *Lark Rise to Candleford*, Oxford University Press, 1945.
2. Lady Augusta Llanover, *The First Principles of Good Cookery*, London 1867.
3. Florence White, *Good Things in England*, Jonathan Cape, 1932.
4. Moreton Shand, *A Book of Food*, Jonathan Cape, 1923.
5. Dorothy Hartley, *Food in England*, Macdonald, 1952, and *The Countryman's England*, Batsford, 1935.
6. Anne Willan, *Great Cooks and Their Recipes: From Taillevent to Escoffier*, Pavilion Books, 1992 and Eugène Herbodeau & Paul Thalamas, *Georges Auguste Escoffier*, Practical Press, 1955.
7. The most famous of Elizabeth David's 'Mediterranean' books are *Book of Mediterranean Food*, John Lehmann, 1950, *Italian Food*, Macdonald, 1954, and *French Provincial Cooking*, Michael Joseph, 1960.
8. Claudia Roden, *A Book of Middle Eastern Food*, Thomas Nelson, 1968.
9. Alan Davidson, *Mediterranean Seafood*, Penguin, 1972.
10. Jane Grigson, *English Food*, Macmillan, 1974.
11. Madhur Jaffrey, *A Taste of India*, Pavilion, 1985.
12. Elizabeth David, *Spices, Salt and Aromatics in the English Kitchen*, Penguin, 1970.

Select Bibliography

Petits Propos culinaires (in English), a specialist journal dealing with many aspects of the history of food, is published three times a year by Prospect Books. Details from: Prospect Books Ltd, 45 Lamont Road, London SW10 0HU.

Abdy, Revd Stodherd, 'A Journal of a Visit in Berkshire, 1770', in A.A. Houblon, *The Houblon Family*, London 1907.

Acton, Eliza, *Modern Cookery for Private Families*, London 1845: facsimile, London 1966.

Adams, S. *The Compleat Servant,* 1825.

Aikin, Lucy, *Memoirs of the Court of Queen Elizabeth*, London 1819.

Arcana Fairfaxiana: facsimile, Newcastle 1894.

Armstrong, L. C., *Modern Etiquette in Public & Private,* London 1887.

Ashmole, Elias, *Institution, Laws and Ceremonies of the Most Noble Order of the Garter*, London 1672.

Auerbach, E. & C. Kingsley Adams, *Paintings and Sculpture at Hatfield House,* London 1971.

Aylett, Mary & Olive Ordish, *First Catch your Hare*, London 1965.

Battiscombe, G., *English Picnics*, London 1949.

Beeton, Isabella, *The Book of Household Management*, London 1861 (1st edition) and 1892 edition.

Bell, Joseph, *A Treatise of Confectionery*, Newcastle 1817.

Benporat, Claudio, *Storia della Gastronomia Italiana*, Milan, 1990.

Bickerdyke, John, *The Curiosities of Ale and Beer* (1889), Spring Books 1965.

Bishop, Frederick, *The Wife's Own Book of Cookery*, London 1862.

Black, M., *Georgian Meals and Menus*, Bath 1977.

Brand, John, *Observations on Popular Antiquities*, London 1807.

The Breakfast Book, London 1865.

Brears, Peter, *Traditional Food in Yorkshire*, Wakefield 1987.
All the King's Cooks, London 1999.
The Gentlewoman's Kitchen, Wakefield 1984.

Brown, Peter, *Pyramids of Pleasure*, York 1990.
Keeping of Christmas, York 1992.
In Praise of Hot Liquour, York 1995.

Brown, Peter & Ivan Day, *The Pleasures of the Table*, York 1997.

Brown, Peter & M. Schwartz, *Come Drink the Bowl Dry*, York 1996.

Buchan, William, *Observations concerning the Diet of the Common People*, London 1797.
Domestic Medicine, London 1803.

Carter, Charles C., *The Compleat Practical Cook*, London 1730.

Chambers, J., *The English House*, London 1985.

Chancellor, E. B., *The Eighteenth Century in London*, London 1920.

Chaney, Lisa, *Elizabeth David*, London 1998.

Charsley, Simon, *Wedding Cakes and Cultural History*, London 1992.

Cobbett, William, *Cottage Economy*, London 1831.

A Collection of Ordinances and Regulations for the Government of the Royal Households, made in Divers Reigns, London 1790.

Cooper, C., *The English Table in History and Literature*, 1929.

Cries of York, York, *c.*1820.

Cromwell, Elizabeth, *The Court and Kitchen of Elizabeth commonly called Joan Cromwell*, London 1664.

David, Elizabeth, *English Bread and Yeast Cookery*, London 1977.
Spices, Salt and Aromatics in the English Kitchen, London 1971.
'Harvest of the Cold Months', in *The Social History of Ice and Ices* (ed. Jill Norman), London 1994.

Davidson, Alan, *Mediterranean Seafood,* Penguin 1972.
The Oxford Companion to Food, Oxford 1999.

Davidson, C., *A Woman's Work is Never Done*, London 1983.
The World of Mary Ellen Best, London 1983.

Day, Ivan, 'Sculpture for the Eighteenth Century Dessert', in *Food in the Arts*, Proceedings of the Oxford Symposium on Food and Cookery, Totnes 1999.

Defoe, Daniel, *Advice and Rules for Servants*, London 1718.

Deloney, Francis, *Jack of Newbury*, London 1633.

Dessert & Sweetmeat Glasses, Country Life, 2 December and 2 February 1944–5.

Diderot, Denis, *Encyclopédie, ou Dictionnaire Raisonné des Sciences, des Arts et des Métiers*, Paris 1763.

Digby, Kenelm, *The Closet of the Eminently Learned Sir Kenelme Digby. Kt. Opened* , London 1671.

Dodsley, R., *The Footman's Friendly Advice to His Brethren of the Livery*, 1729.

Driver, Christopher, *John Evelyn, Cook*, Totnes 1997.

Drummond, J.C. & Anne Wilbraham, *The Englishman's Food: Five centuries of English diet*, London 1957.

Earle, P., *A City full of People*, London 1994.
Ellis, William. *The Country Housewife's Family Companion*, London 1750.
Emmerson, R, *British Teapots and Tea drinking 1700-1850*, HMSO, London, 1992
Estienne, Charles, *Maison Rustique, or the Countrey Farme. Compyled in the French Tongue by Charles Stevens and John Liebault, and translated into English by Richard Surfleet. Reviewed, corrected and augmented by Gervase Markham*, London 1616.
Evelyn, John, *Acetaria*, London 1699.

Frith, W.P., *My Autobiography and Reminiscences*, London 1887.
Garway, Thomas, *An Exact Description of the Growth, Quality, and Vertues of the Leaf Tee, alias Tay*, London 1660.
Geddes, Olive M., *The Laird's Kitchen*, Edinburgh 1994.
Girouard, Mark, *Life in the English Country House*, New Haven and London 1978.
A Country House Companion, London 1987.
Glass Circle, Vols 1 & 2, Newcastle 1972–5.
Glasse, H., *The Art of Cookery*, London 1747.
The Servants Directory, London 1760.
The Complete Confectioner, London 1762.
Granville, M., *Life & Correspondence of Mrs. Delany*, ed. Lady Llanover, London 1861–2.
Grigson, Geoffrey, *The Englishman's Flora*, London 1958.
Grigson, Jane, *English Food*, London 1974.
Hake, E., *Newes out of Powles Churchyard*, London 1579.
Harding, S., *The Behaviour of Servants in England*, London 1724.
Harland, John (ed.), *The Home and Farm Accounts of the Shuttleworths of Gawthorpe*, Chetham 1868.
Hartley, Dorothy, *The Countryman's England*, London 1935.
Food in England, London 1954.
Hayward, A., *The Art of Dining*, London 1883.
Herbodeau, Eugène & Paul Thalamas, *Georges Auguste Escoffier*, London 1955.
Hess, Karen, *Martha Washington's Booke of Cookery*, New York 1981.
Hibbert, C., *George IV*, London 1975.
Holinshed, R., Chronicles, vol. I: *The Description and Historie of England written by WH*, London 1587.
Houlbrooke, R., *English Family Life, 1576–1716*, Oxford 1989.
Hughes, G.B., 'The Old English Banquet', *Country Life*, 17 February 1955.
Irvine, L., *Royal Doulton Bunnykins Collectors Book*, Richard Dennis, London 1984.
Jack, F., *The Woman's Book*, London 1911.
Jaffrey, Madhur, *A Taste of India*, Pavilion 1985.
James, J., *The Memoirs of a House Steward*, London 1949.
Kelsall, K., *Glass in 18th Century England: The Footed Salver*, Exeter 1989.
Kenney, Herbert A., *Picnics and Suppers*, London 1901.
Kettilby, M., *A Collection of Receipts in Cookery, Physick and Surgery*, London 1728.
Kidder, Edward, *Receipts in Pastry & Cookery*, London c.1720.
Kitchener, William, *The Cook's Oracle*, London 1823.
La Chapelle, V., *Le Cuisinier moderne*, The Hague 1742.
Lamb, Patrick, *Royal Cookery*, London 1710.
Landon, Major James Henry, *Breakfasts, Luncheons, and Ball Suppers*, London 1887.
Laurioux, Bruno, *Le Règne de Taillevent*, Paris 1997.
Lehmann, Gilly, *The English Housewife*, Totnes 2000.
Letters of Lady Rachel Russell, London 1773.
Leyel, Mrs C. F., *Picnics for Motorists*, London 1936.
Liddell, Caroline & Robin Weir, *Ices, the Definitive Guide*, London 1998.
Llanover, Lady Augusta, *The First Principles of Good Cookery*, London 1867.
MacDonald, J., *Memoirs of an 18th Century Footman*, London 1790.
Maclean, Virginia, *A Short Title Catalogue of Household and Cookery Books published in the English Tongue 1701-1800*, London 1981.
Markham, Gervase, *The English Housewife*, London 1615.
Mason, Laura, *Sugar Plums and Sherbet: The Prehistory of Sweets*, Totnes 1998.
(with Catherine Brown) *Traditional Foods of Britain: an Inventory*, Totnes 1999.
'Everything stops for Tea', in C. Anne Wilson (ed.), *Luncheon, Nuncheon and Other Meals*, Stroud 1994.
Massialot, F., *The Court and Country Cook*, London 1702.
Mathews, *The Family Instructor*, London 1715.
May, Robert, *The Accomplisht Cook, or the Art and Mystery of Cookery*, 1660: facsimile of 1685 edition, Totnes 1994.
Mayhew, Henry, *The Morning Chronicle Survey of Labour and the Poor*, new edn, London 1980.
Mennell, S., *All Manners of Food*, London 1985.
Moufet, Thomas, *Healths Improvement*, London 1633.
Murdie, R., *A Historical Account of His Majesty's visit to Scotland*, Edinburgh 1822.
Murrell, John, *A Daily Exercise for Ladies and Gentlewomen*, London 1617.
Murrell, John, *Murrels Two Books of Cookerie and Carving*, 1638: facsimile, Ilkley 1985.
Nichols, J., *Progresses and Public Processions of James I*, London 1828.
Northumberland Household Book: The Regulations and Establishment of the Household of Henry Algernon Percy 1512, new edn, - London 1905.
Nott, John, *The Cook's and Confectioner's Dictionary*, London 1723.
Nugent, M., *Lady Nugent's Journal of Her Residence in Jamaica 1801-1805*, London 1810.
Nutt, Frederick, *The Compleat Confectioner*, London 1789.

Oliver, G., 'Old Christmas customs and popular superstitions of Lincolnshire', *Gentleman's Magazine*, London 1832, CII, pp.491–4.
Oxford, Arnold Whitaker, *English Cookery Books to the Year 1850* (1913), London 1979.

Paidagogos, *More Hints on Etiquette*, London 1865.
Palmer, Arnold, *Movable Feasts*, Oxford 1952.
Movable Feasts – changes in English eating habits, Oxford 1984.
Parkinson, John, *Theatrum Botanicum*, London 1640.
Peacock, Alfred, *Bread and Blood*, London 1965.
Puttenham, William, *The Art of English Poesie*, London 1589.
Pyne, W. H., *Royal Residences*, London 1819.
Quayle, E., *Old Cook Books*, London 1978.
Rabisha, William, *The Whole Body of Cookery Dissected*, London 1661.
Raffald, E., *The Experienced English Housekeeper*, 1st edn, 1769.
Raines, Robert, *Marcellus Laroon*, London 1967.
Riley, Gillian, *A Feast for the Eyes*, London 1997.
'Tainted Meat', in *Spicing up the Palate*, Proceedings of the Oxford Symposium on Food and Cookery, Totnes 1993.
Roden, Claudia, *A Book of Middle Eastern Food*, London 1968.
Rose, Giles, *A Perfect School of Instructions for the Officers of the Mouth*, London 1682.
Rowntree, B. Seebohm, *Poverty: A Study of Town Life*, London 1901.
Ruscelli, Girolamo, *The Secretes of Maister Alexis of Piedmont*, London 1558.
St-Fond, F. de, *Travels in England and Scotland*, 1789.
Salmon, William, *The New London Dispensatory*, London 1690.
The Family Dictionary, London 1710.
Sambrook, Pamela A. & Peter Brears, *The Country House Kitchen 1650–1900*, Stroud 1997.
Sandford, Francis, *History of the Coronation of James II*, London 1687.
Scappi, Bartolomeo, *Opera*, 1570: facsimile, Bologna 1981.
Scarfe, Norman (tr. & ed.), *A Frenchman's Year in Suffolk 1784*, Woodbridge 1988.
Shand, Moreton, *A Book of Food*, Jonathan Cape 1923.
Shuckman, C. & D. De Hoop Scheffer, *Dutch and Flemish Etchings, Engravings and Woodcuts c.1450–1700*, Rosendal, 1991.
Smith, E. C., *The Compleat Housewife*, London 1730.
Solkin, D., 'Vauxhall Gardens', in *Painting for Money*, New Haven 1995.
Soyer, A., *The Gastronomic Regenerator*, London 1846.
Spurling, Hilary, *Elinor Fettiplace's Receipt Book*, London 1986.
Stubbes, Philip, *Anatomie of Abuses*, London 1583.
Swift, J., *Directions to Servants*, London 1745.
Sykes, C. S., *Private Palaces*, London 1985.
Tannahill, Reay, *Food in History*, London 1973.
Tharp, L., *Hogarth's China*, London 1997.
Thick, M., *The Neat House Gardens*, Totnes 1998.
Thomas, C., *The Footman's Directory*, 2nd edn, London 1825.
Thompson, Flora, *Lark Rise to Candleford*, London 1946.
Tierney, J. J., *The Celtic Ethnography of Posidonius*, London 1960.
The True Way of Preserving and Candying..., 1695: facsimile, Ilkley 1994.
Trussler, J., *The Honours of the Table*, London 1788.
Tryon, Thomas, *The Good House-wife made a Doctor*, London 1692.
Turbervile, *The Noble Arte of Venerie*, London 1567.
Ukers, W.H., *All About Tea*, London 1935.
Walpole, Horace, *Correspondence*, New Haven 1941.
Walton, J. K., *Fish and Chips and the British Working Class – 1870–1940*, Leicester 1992.
Wells-Cole, Anthony, *Art and Decoration in Elizabethan and Jacobean England*, Yale University Press, 1997.
Whatman, S., *The Housekeeping Book*, reprint, London 1983.
Wheaton, B. K., *Savouring the Past*, London 1983.
White, Florence, *Good Things in England*, London 1932.
White, T. H., *The Age of Scandal*, Oxford 1986.
The Whole Duty of a Woman, London 1737.
Willan, Anne, *Great Cooks and their Recipes. From Taillevent to Escoffier*, London 1992.
Wilson, C. Anne, *Food and Drink in Britain, From the Stone Age to Recent Times*, London 1973.
(ed.), *Banquetting Stuffe*, Edinburgh 1990.
(ed.), *The Appetite and the Eye*, Edinburgh 1991.
W. M., *The Queens Closet Open'd*, London 1655: facsimile, London 1984.
The Women's Petition against Coffee, London n.d., *c.*1674.
Woodforde J., *Diary of a Country Parson 1758–1802*.
Wynken de Worde, *The Boke of Kervynge*, London 1508.

Glossary

Space allows only brief definitions of specialist words mentioned in the text. For more complete treatments of archaic and unusual culinary terms, see Alan Davidson, The Oxford Companion to Food, *Oxford University Press, 1999, and Karen Hess,* Martha Washington's Booke of Cookery, *Columbia University Press, 1981.*

ale barm The yeast-rich froth skimmed from the top of fermenting ale or beer, formerly used as a leaven for raising bread and cake dough.

ambergris A sweet-scented material produced in the gut of the sperm whale, used in perfumery as a fixative. Until the seventeenth century it was also popular as a flavouring, particularly in confectionery (see **musk**).

ambigue (more correctly **ambigu**) A type of baroque court meal in which both courses and the dessert were set out on the table at the same time. Many designs for elaborate ambigues are given in Carter, *The Compleat Practical Cook*.

annok An extinct name for a type of oat or barley cake.

assiette montée An inedible table decoration made from pasteboard with a wirework superstructure – not to be confused with a *pièce montée*, a culinary sculpture contrived from sugar paste or other food materials.

banquet This word has two shades of meaning. Today we use it to describe a grand formal celebratory meal. In the sixteenth, seventeenth and early eighteenth centuries a banquet was also the name for the sweet after-course of the meal. It was frequently served in a purpose-built banqueting house.

banqueting stuffe (banqueting matters) Elizabethan and Jacobean terms for dessert foods and drink: comfits, spiced wine, liqueurs, cream cheeses and dairy foods such as syllabubs and trifles.

barberries The fruits of the British native barberry (*Berberis vulgaris* L.). An important garnish and source of acid flavouring in English cookery until the late eighteenth century, when it was discovered to be a vector of wheat rust and ceased to be cultivated. In the sixteenth century a variety with large fruits, known as the nutmeg barberry, was used to garnish boiled pike at London livery feasts. Barberries were also preserved in syrup (frequently in bunches) and in the eighteenth century used to flavour ice cream.

barm see **ale barm**.

battalia pie – probably from French *béatilles* (titbits) A raised pie filled with a complex mixture of offal and small tidbits such as sweetbreads, lamb testicles, larks, oysters, chestnuts and barberries. It was also used to describe a mixed fish pie made in the form of a crenellated castle. The pastry battlements were garnished with stuffed fish heads! Both types of pie, though medieval in origin, are typical of seventeenth-century court cookery.

bawned herring – origin of 'bawned' obscure but may mean gently poached, probably from *bawne*, a variant of *balne* from Latin *balneum* (bath) A bain-marie or double boiler is the kitchen version of the apothecary's *balneum marium*, a waterbath used for the gentle distillation of oils and spirits.

bever – also **bœuer** or **beaver** from Old French *beivre* (to drink) A small snack between meals accompanied by a drink (see also **nuncheon**).

bisque (also **bisk**) A complex mixed stew of game or fish of continental origin. A spectacular dish in seventeenth-century court meals, where similar festival foods from southern Europe, such as olios (*olla podrida*) and terrines, were frequently presented as ostentatious centrepieces during the first course.

blancmange (sometimes **blanmanger**) – from Old French *blanc mangier*/Italian *biancomangiare* (white food) Originally a delicate blend of minced capon breast, ground almonds and cream flavoured with rosewater. It eventually evolved into a simple cream or milk jelly and came to form the basis of many eighteenth-century edible table ornaments moulded in the form of fish, eggs in a nest of lemon zest or even Solomon's Temple. Sometimes also called **flummery**.

bohea In the eighteenth century this term described the finest grade of black tea from the Wu-I shan range in northern Fuhkien.

botargo Salted and pressed mullet's roe in the form of a sausage, imported from southern Europe. Popular among seventeenth-century imbibers (including Pepys) as a thirst-inducer.

brooklime (*Veronica beccabunga* L.) A common plant of pond and stream margins, used in traditional herbal medicine as a specific against scurvy and for this reason formerly included in spring salads.

bustard (*Otix tarda*) A large, mainly terrestrial, bird hunted into extinction in Britain in the mid-nineteenth century.

capon A castrated cockerel.

caudle Originally a hot spicy drink of ale or wine whisked into an emulsion with egg yolks. During the seventeenth century it also came to mean a sauce made of sack, butter and eggs for pouring into pies. This type was sometimes called a **lear**.

charger A large serving dish or plate.

cheat (also **cheate** or **chet**) A form of wholemeal or brown bread considered to be of secondary quality, after manchet. Sometimes called trencher bread as it was used to make bread trenchers.

Clarenceux A principal officer of the Knights of the Garter. He was the second King-of-Arms in England, whose chief role was to arrange the funerals of all knights living south of the river Trent. Sometimes also called Surroy (Norroy being his northern counterpart).

cock's combs (also written as **cockscombs**) The fleshy, usually red, combs from the heads of domestic cockerels. Much used in seventeenth- and eighteenth-century court cookery as a garnish. When boiled they lose their red colour and turn a bleached white.

cock's stones (also written as **cock stones**) Cockerels' testicles.

comfits An ancient form of sweet made by coating seeds, spices and nuts with sugar. Their primary use seems to have been medicinal, but they rapidly became a luxury treat and were associated with rites of passage and celebrations such as weddings and christenings.

comport (from French *compotier*) A dessert dish on a raised support.

compotes Freshly stewed or poached fruits served in syrup.

conceit A novelty table ornament made from food materials such as almond paste or sugar paste, in the form of an animal, heraldic motif or architectural feature (see also **marchpane** and **soteltie**).

cordials Strong alcoholic waters distilled over herbs or other substances with alleged beneficial effects on the heart. Early cordial waters sometimes contained flecks of gold leaf, ground pearls and 'cardiac' herbs like sundew and bugloss.

cotoniac (also spelt **cotoniack**, **cotoniake**, **quiddoniak**, etc.) Quince paste. An important element in the banquet course, this thick paste or jelly-like confection was frequently printed with ornamental designs and stored in round wooden boxes. Various forms imported from France and southern Europe were eventually imitated by English housewives from the late sixteenth century onwards (see also **quiddany** and **marmalet**).

crowdi In seventeenth- and eighteenth-century Scotland and northern England, regional name for a type of oatmeal porridge.

dessert frame A kind of ornamental platform for raising a display of dessert foods above the level of the table. Precursors of the *surtout de table* and mirror-glass plateau of the eighteenth century, the earliest dessert frames seem to have been made of wood, often edged with basketwork and frequently gilded.

dole A distribution of alms, usually of bread and other basic food.

dry confections Candied fruits, comfits, biscuits, etc.

eggs of Portugal Portugal was celebrated during the seventeenth century for complex confections made from eggs and egg yolks, recipes for which were included in some English cookery books of the time.

ewer An ornamental pitcher or jug-like vessel, usually made from a precious metal and used for pouring rosewater or other scented water onto the hands at the end of the meal, over a similarly ornamental basin. Until the seventeenth century it was also the title of the officer responsible for overseeing the washing of the sovereign's hands.

flummery (from Welsh *llymru*) Originally a jelly-like dish made by steeping oatmeal in water. From the eighteenth century onwards more usually a sweet cream jelly set with isinglass, hartshorn, shaved ivory or calves' foot jelly. The equivalent of modern **blancmange**.

flux An early name for dysentery.

fricandeaux A dish of French origin, frequent in English cookery books from the early eighteenth century onwards. Usually thin slices (collops) of veal or other meats, **larded** with bacon fat and cooked gently in a closed stewpan.

frumenty (or **furmety**) – from Latin *frumentum* (grain) A very ancient dish of hulled wheat boiled in milk and sweetened with sugar. In medieval times a traditional accompaniment to porpoise at important court feasts, this glutinous wheat porridge was also eaten in northern England by the less well-off as a Christmas dish until the nineteenth century.

galantine In medieval cookery, a jellied sauce of fish or pork. Chaucer mentions 'pike in galantine'. At the time of George IV, more likely pressed veal or boned suckling pig coated in aspic jelly.

Garter The principal 'King' of Arms and Heralds (see also **Clarenceux**).

girdbrew An extinct form of oatmeal porridge.

grosses entrées Complicated mixed stews such as **bisques**, olios and terrines. These elaborately garnished and strongly seasoned stews were the principal dishes of the first course of court meals in the seventeenth and early eighteenth centuries.

haggis Although it has only survived in Scotland into modern times, haggis or haggister pudding was also once commonly eaten in England and seems to have been particularly popular in the seventeenth century. The earliest recipes occur in early fifteenth-century English court cookery books. A sweet haggis known as a hackin or hack pudding was served in the Lake District as a Christmas breakfast dish until the mid-nineteenth century. A similar sweet haggis survives in Aberdeenshire.

havercake (from Old Norse *hafri* – oats) An extinct term for various forms of oatcake from the Central and North Pennines.

hippocras (or **hypocras**) A very sweet spiced wine served at the void or banquet. It probably derived its name from *manicum hippocraticum* (the sleeve of Hippocrates) – an apothecary's term for a woollen filter used to strain out the spice particles from the gyle (the mixture of wine and spice). Among the spices included in hippocras gyle mixtures were cinnamon, long pepper, cubebs and grains of paradise.

huckaback (sometimes **hagabag**) A strong diaper or linen fabric used for table cloths and napkins.

jannock (or **ianack**) A form of leavened oat or barley cake, formerly made in the North of England. In his *Healths Improvement* (1633) Thomas Moufet tells us: 'Had Galen seen the Oaten Cakes of the North, the Janocks of Lancashire, and the Grues of Cheshire, he would have confessed that Oats and Oatmeal are not only Meat for Beasts, but also for tall, fair and strong Men and Women.'

jumbalds (more usually **jumbles** or **jumballs**) A type of biscuit in the form of an elaborate knot. In France they were known as *gimblettes* and were usually boiled in a kettle before being baked in an oven. They belonged to an ancient family of baked goods that included cracknels, simnels, **turtulongs** and bagels. Jumbles were also made from quince and pippin paste.

lamb's stones Lambs' testicles.

lamprey (*Petromyzon marinus*) A primitive parasitic fish much valued in the seventeenth century, but rarely eaten today other than in parts of Gloucestershire .

larded Because the strong radiant heat given off by a great roasting range could dry out delicate cuts of meat and poultry, they were often 'larded', i.e. small strips of fat – **lardoons** – were threaded through the flesh to keep it moist. This was frequently done in a decorative manner, almost like embroidery, and materials such as strips of orange peel and pickled cucumber were also used. In the seventeenth century dry fish (for example, pike) were larded with strips of eel or anchovy.

lear, see **caudle**

liquid sweetmeats Preserved fruits (or fruit peels) in syrup or brandy served at the banquet or dessert. More generally the term could also include jams, jellies, syllabubs and other cream dishes.

loblolly A buttered oatmeal porridge eaten by Elizabethan seafarers.

manchet Bread rolls, usually weighing six ounces, baked from the finest quality of white flour. Moufet refers to them as gentlemens' rolls.

mangoes Pickled and preserved mangoes were imported into England in the seventeenth century. They were probably very expensive and counterfeit mangoes were made from cucumbers.

maraskino (maraschino) A liqueur distilled from cherries, particularly popular as a flavouring in confectionery and ices at the time of the Prince Regent – a vital ingredient in *Punch Romaine*, a luxurious water ice based on meringue, brandy and champagne.

marchpane Usually a large disc of almond paste dried slowly in an oven and decorated with various 'standards' or devices, including animals or heraldic emblems made from sugar paste or marzipan. Frequently gilded and 'struck' with long comfits or gilded date stones. Marchpanes evolved from medieval **sotelties** and were usually used as centrepieces at sixteenth- and seventeenth-century banquets.

marmalet (marmalade) Unlike modern jam-like marmalades, this was a thick fruit paste made usually from quinces, but also from other fruits, including oranges (see also **cotoniac** and **quidanny**).

maslin (Old French *mesteillon*) A mixed grain bread usually of rye and wheat, particularly common in the North-East of England until the early nineteenth century. Sometimes called monk's corne or monkecorne bread.

mess A serving of dishes, usually for four people.

morels (*Morchella esculenta*) An edible fungus much used in seventeenth- and eighteenth-century court cookery as a garnish and in various made dishes.

musk A crystalline substance with a powerful persistent odour, obtained from the anal gland of the musk deer (*Moschus moschiferus*). In the sixteenth and seventeenth centuries much used as a flavouring, particularly in confectionery and for scenting hippocras.

muskadine A spiced wine related to **hippocras**, seemingly popular at weddings and christening celebrations. One kind was made by mixing reduced wine (known to English vintners as *soot*) with sack and spices.

noyeau A syrup or liqueur flavoured with bitter almonds or peach or apricot kernels.

nuncheon – Middle English *noneshench* (literally, noon drink) A light midday snack. The word is the origin of the more recent term luncheon.

orris A sweet scented powder made from the ground rhizomes of *Iris fiorintina*. It was used to make *nonpareils* – the tiny comfits we now call 'hundreds and thousands'.

parterres Miniature parterres made of various materials including coloured sugars were frequently used to embellish dessert plateaux between *c.*1740 and *c.*1820 (see also **dessert frame**).

patties Small fried or baked filled pastries used for garnishing.

peason Garden peas.

plateau A slightly elevated platform made of mirrored glass, sometimes with separate and movable silver or gilt frames. Used for laying out the foods and ornaments of the dessert course in the eighteenth century (see also **dessert frame** and **parterres**).

poddish A Cumberland and Westmorland dialect name for porridge.

ponche à la Régence George IV's favourite punch recipe. It was flavoured with citron and vanilla and was drunk as an accompaniment to turtle soup.

prebends Pensioners of the Order of the Garter.

prelates Principal officers of the Order of the Garter.

quiddany A fruit paste or jelly-like marmalade.

ragou (sometimes **ragout**, from French *ragoûter* – to refresh) A slowly cooked stew of vegetables and meat that was 'refreshed' with an extravagant and richly flavoured sauce called a cullis (*coulis*) at the end of the cooking time. Typical of early eighteenth-century court cookery.

remove A principal dish of the first course that was used to fill the space left after the removal of the soup tureen.

ruff (*Machetes pugnax*) A male sandpiper; the female was called a reeve. Recipes for ruffs and reeves occur frequently in English cookery books until the early nineteenth century.

sack A much-disputed word, but a general term for strong white wines imported from Spain and the Canary Islands.

Sewer – probably from French *asseoir* (to seat) The principal officer at a court meal who superintended the seating arrangements, table layout and distribution of food.

shagreen An untanned leather of a dark colour, frequently green.

soteltie (also **subtiltie**) An ornamental dish or entertainment at a medieval or sixteenth century feast, usually with some allegorical significance (see also **marchpane**).

soup à la Reine A meat soup of French court origin, thickened with pulverized almonds.

sucket – from French *succade* (juicy) Wet suckets were preserved fruits in syrup, usually citrus peels. Dry suckets were candied and dried fruits. (See also **liquid sweetmeats** and **dry confections**.)

trencher – from French *trancher* (to cut or slice) Originally a rectangular cutting pad made from four-day-old cheat bread on which diners sliced their meat. During the sixteenth century they were made from wood and frequently had a small round indentation for salt. Fruit trenchers, posies or roundels were elaborately decorated wooden trenchers used at the banquet course.

truffle (*Tuber melanosporum*) An edible subterranean fungus imported into England from France in the seventeenth century and used, or allegedly used, in court cookery.

turtulong A breakfast roll of the *gimblette* variety (see **jumbalds**), which appears to have enjoyed a brief vogue in late eighteenth-century London.

umbles (sometimes **numbles**) Deer's offal.

venison pasty Venison baked in a thick pastry usually made of rye meal. Venison baked in this way could be kept for a long time, as the hard crust is impenetrable to bacteria. These pasties were frequently sent long distances as presents, especially for wedding feasts.

voidée (sometimes **void**) – from French *voider* (to clear away) The closing ritual of a medieval or Renaissance court meal, which took place just before the table was cleared. The diners were offered hippocras, wafers and comfits.

voiding basket A shallow basket used to clear away the leftovers after the meal.

washbrew An archaic form of oatmeal porridge.

wet suckets, see **suckets**

wiggs (also **whigs**, **wigs**, **wigges**) Small leavened sweet buns flavoured with caraway seeds or comfits. In the Lake counties they were served at funeral feasts.

Index